Circa 1945, Age 60

BESS WALLACE TRUMAN

February 13, 1885 – October 20, 1982
Married Harry S. Truman, June 28, 1919
Daughter, Margaret

The purpose of Junior Service League of Independence, Missouri shall be to arouse interest among its members in the social, economic, educational, cultural, and civic conditions of the community, and to prepare them for intelligent participation in activities of value to the community.

The proceeds realized from the sale of *The Bess Collection* will be used to support community projects in our area.

Copies of *The Bess Collection* may be obtained from
The Independence Junior Service League
P.O. Box 1571
Independence, MO 64055

ISBN 0-9615328-0-7
Copyright © 1993
Junior Service League of Independence, Missouri
All Rights Reserved

First printing: 3,000 copies, June 1993
Second printing: 3,000 copies, November 1993
Third printing: 5,000 copies, September 1995

Printed in the USA by

WIMMER
The Wimmer Companies, Inc.
Memphis

All recipes herein have been tested and represent favorite recipes of Junior Service League members, their relatives and friends. Brand names of ingredients have been used only when necessary.

The divider page recipes are original to Mrs. Truman and reflect cooking practices of her era.

The Bess Collection

TOP: Bess Wallace (seated on the floor) relaxes with her family in the parlor of 219 N. Delaware in this early photo. Left to right: Bess's mother, Madge Gates Wallace; probably her brothers, George and Frank Wallace; and an unidentified man (possibly one of Madge's brothers).

ABOVE: Bess, left, with life-long friend Mary Paxton.

Bess Wallace Truman never wanted to be our nation's first lady. Indeed, some people called her a reluctant politician's wife. She shied away from the limelight and dreaded public intrusions into her private affairs. Throughout Bess's ninety-seven years, family and friends were the focus of her life—a life enriched by her love of learning, letter writing and sports.

The eldest daughter of a longtime Independence family, Bess grew up in a fashionable neighborhood on North Delaware Street. Her grandfather, George Porterfield Gates, founded the first commercial flour mill in Missouri. He built the white frame house where Bess grew up, raised her daughter and eventually retired with Harry.

Her parents named her Elizabeth Virginia Wallace, but people called the young blue-eyed blonde "Bessie" for short. Her family

BELOW: Bess makes a face at younger brother Fred while they enjoy a sunny afternoon with brothers Frank and George.

ABOVE: Bess Wallace portrays the "best man" (third from right), while staging a wedding with some friends (quite likely members of her Cadiz Club).

entertained the finest social groups in the city. Status was important to her mother, Madge Gates Wallace, who once scolded Bess for helping a servant hang out the wash to dry.

Bess was a well-mannered child who always dressed in the newest fashions. She loved to read. She danced, ice-skated, fished and rode horses. She had a terrific tennis stroke and threw a baseball better than many boys. In fact, she once rescued her brothers' team from sure defeat in a sandlot game. Losing by three runs in the last inning, the brothers recruited Bess to pinch hit with the bases loaded. She promptly lashed a home run and got a good dress dirty in the process.

When Bess was eighteen years old, the handsome father she adored took his own life. The tragedy made a wreck of her mother, who became a recluse, and Bess accepted the responsibility of taking charge of the family. A close friend and neighbor, Mary Paxton, helped Bess through this difficult time. Just months earlier, Bess had consoled Mary when her mother died of tuberculosis. They understood each other's grief very well.

With her husband gone, Madge Gates Wallace became highly protective of her only daughter. She set high standards for Bess's beaus. It became clear that any suitor would need to spend a lot of time with Bess's mother.

ABOVE: Mrs. Allen Prewitt, Julie Rugg, Anna Prewitt and Bess Wallace visit the 1911 Independence, Missouri Fair.

Bess was very popular with the boys. To narrow the field of suitors, she devised an unusual test whereby she would take them on an extremely long walk and picnic. Such an outing gave Bess the chance to study a man closely—out of the watchful gaze of her mother and away from the influence of her friends. Bess particularly liked one Kansas City man, Julian Harvey, but he failed her "test." Later, Harry Truman, the son of a Grandview farmer, would "pass."

Harry and Bess had been acquainted since childhood. In fact, Harry had been smitten with Bess since he was six years old and saw her for the first time in a Sunday School class. Bess paid little attention to him. It wasn't until 1910, nine years after they graduated from high school together, that they sat down for their first long conversation. That evening, an eager Harry Truman had appeared on Bess's doorstep to return a cake plate from his cousins' house across the street.

Harry began an earnest courtship, but Bess turned down his first proposal of marriage. She changed her mind a few years later, and the couple waited for Harry to succeed in a business before getting married. World War I interrupted their plans, and the two grew even more fond of each other while separated by the cold waters of the Atlantic Ocean.

On June 28, 1919—after nine years of dating and shortly after Captain Truman returned from war—they married at Trinity Episcopal Church. Bess was 34, Harry, 35. They went to Chicago on their honeymoon, then they moved in with Bess's mother, who thought Harry never would amount to much.

After the war, Harry tried several unsuccessful ventures, including opening a men's store. Bess kept the books and handled the advertising. Eventually, she would letter its final CLOSED sign. The financial stress took a toll on Bess, who suffered two miscarriages and feared she was becoming too old to have a child. Finally, on February 17, 1924—four days after Bess's 39th birthday— Mary Margaret Truman arrived.

BELOW: After two miscarriages, Bess was especially happy with the birth of Margaret in 1924.

Harry had become involved in local politics and enjoyed some success. Bess kept a close tab on political issues, but she much preferred staying home with Margaret to attending political functions. After many years as a successful county politician, Harry was elected to the United States Senate. He gained national prominence in Washington, and Franklin Delano Roosevelt selected Harry as his running mate in 1944. Bess was unprepared for the increased attention of the media—attention that soon would increase dramatically.

Bess sobbed when she learned that FDR had died, just 82 days after Harry had become vice president. She sobbed even longer that night, after Harry was sworn in as the nation's 33rd president. But as she did when her father died, she put aside her own feelings and filled her new role.

ABOVE: Bess was always there for her mother, Madge Gates Wallace, shown here in 1949, in her room at Blair House, Washington, D.C.

As time passed, Bess's pleasant demeanor and concern for others made her a favorite among politicians and White House regulars. Harry took to calling her "the boss," but she didn't like it when people made a fuss over her. During her first visit to her Independence bridge club after she became first lady, she scolded the group for standing at her arrival. According to written accounts, she said, "Now stop it, stop it this instant. Sit down, every darn one of you." Later, members of the bridge club would be honored guests at the White House.

Many people requested recipes from Bess while she was first lady. One of the favorites, Ozark pudding, created a stir when a Virginia woman complained that it turned out so terrible her family refused to eat it. Food specialists tested the recipe and proclaimed it fine. Another time, the same recipe was published with a mistake in the ingredients, and another fracas ensued. Upset, Bess refused to give out the recipe again.

During the White House years, people described Bess as down-to-earth, the "spark plug" of the family, shy, sincere and kind, with a "rollicking sense of humor." She often told the servants to stop working so hard. She dressed simply and never was pretentious. She insisted on remaining in the background and shunned the tradition of weekly press conferences initiated by her predecessor, Eleanor Roosevelt. When Harry decided not to seek re-election in 1952, Bess was the happiest person in the White House.

Harry and Bess lived out their lives in the quiet of their white frame house at 219 North Delaware Street. (Secret Service agents established a post in the house across the street.) Harry died in 1972. After Bess died in 1982, Margaret found hundreds of letters her mother had saved from Harry and others, including Mary Paxton. The value Bess placed on these letters exemplifies how much family and friends meant to her throughout her long life.

The Junior Service League of Independence is proud to present this cookbook in loving memory of Bess Wallace Truman.

BELOW: Bess relaxes with President Truman and Margaret on the lawn of the little White House in Key West, Florida, November, 1948. Their private times together were dearly treasured by the Trumans.

Circa 1888, Age 3

Mrs. Truman's Punch

4 quarts grape juice
3 quarts ginger ale
1 quart lemon juice
3 gallons water
  Sugar to taste

Keep cool by using a 2 quart brick of Lemon Ice in the punch bowl. Yield: 5 gallons. Serves 160.

Mrs. Truman's Fruit Punch

1 pint lemon juice
3 quarts orange juice
2 quarts ginger ale
2 quarts White Rock
1 gallon water
1 pint white grape juice
  Sugar to taste

Yield: 3 gallons. Serves 100.

ABOVE: Bess's Independence bridge club posed for this photo at Basswood, in Platte County, in June, 1946. The wooded retreat was made available to the club for its meetings by owner A. J. Stephens, brother-in-law of club member Edna Hutchison. From left, standing, are Bess Truman, Natalie Wallace, Martha Jane Wright, Lucy Peters, Grace Minor, Edna Hutchison, Mary Shaw, Thelma Pallette, May Wallace, Linda King, Adelaide Twyman and Mag Noel. Seated in front are Mary Shaw "Shawsie" Branton, left, and Margaret Truman.

BELOW: The back porch of the Truman home, 219 North Delaware was the site of this 1953 game of canasta. Left to right are May Wallace, Bess Truman, Edna Hutchison and Natalie Wallace.

Crystal Reception Punch

5 cups sugar

2 (12 oz.) cans frozen lemonade

2 cups fresh or bottled lemon juice

5 qts. plus 2 cups water

2 qts. ginger ale, chilled

In a punch bowl, combine sugar, lemonade, lemon juice, and water. Stir until sugar is dissolved.

Refrigerate for several hours to chill.

When ready to serve, add ginger ale.

NOTE: This is a nice clear punch, but if color is desired, food coloring may be added.

YIELD: 10 quarts or 80 (4-ounce) servings

Ruby Almond Punch

4 cups cranberry juice

½ cup sugar

4 cups pineapple juice

1 Tbsp. almond extract

1 (2 liter) bottle ginger ale, chilled

In a punch bowl, combine the cranberry juice, sugar, pineapple juice, and almond extract. Stir until sugar is dissolved.

Refrigerate for several hours to chill.

Just before serving, add ginger ale.

YIELD: 2 quarts or 16 (4-ounce) servings

Strawberry Peach Wine Cooler

1 cup strawberries, sliced

1 cup peaches, chopped

2 Tbsp. sugar

1 bottle white wine, chilled

1 qt. sparkling water, chilled

Mint sprigs, optional

Ice

In a small bowl, combine strawberries and peaches. Sprinkle with sugar; stir gently. Let stand at room temperature 30 minutes.

Pour fruit into punch bowl. Gently pour in wine and sparkling water.

Add mint sprigs and ice.

NOTE: For a non-alcoholic cooler, use only 1 tablespoon sugar. Substitute 1 quart apple juice for wine.

YIELD: 2 quarts or 16 (4-ounce) servings

Cold Duck Punch

1 (12 oz.) can frozen orange juice

1 (12 oz.) can frozen lemonade

1 (12 oz.) can frozen limeade

1 (46 oz.) can pineapple juice

¾ cup sugar, optional

1 (2 liter) bottle ginger ale, chilled

1 bottle Cold Duck, chilled

In a punch bowl, mix frozen orange juice, lemonade, limeade, and pineapple juice. Add sugar, if desired. Refrigerate until ready to serve.

Add chilled ginger ale and Cold Duck just before serving.

YIELD: 8 quarts or 64 (4-ounce) servings

Champagne Punch

½ cup sugar

1 cup hot water

6 oz. lemon juice

2 oz. Maraschino cherry liqueur

2 oz. Curacao or Triple Sec

4 oz. brandy

1 bottle champagne

1 bottle Rhine wine, chilled

2 bottles carbonated water, chilled

1 strawberry ring mold

In a small container, dissolve the sugar in the hot water and add the lemon juice. This may be done ahead of time and chilled.

In the punch bowl, combine the lemon mixture with the next six ingredients.

Add ring mold to keep chilled for serving.

NOTE: This is a powerful punch, so be careful.

• 8 ounces of berries may be added to the punch instead of the strawberry ring mold.

YIELD: 8 quarts

Fruited Champagne Kir

1 lb. fresh
   cranberries
4 cups water
1 (10 oz.) pkg.
   frozen, sweetened
   raspberries
1¼ cups sugar
½ cup Creme
   de Cassis
1 bottle champagne

Combine cranberries and water in a large, heavy saucepan. Bring to a boil. Reduce heat and cook until cranberries are tender. Add the raspberries and cook for 10–15 minutes.

Transfer mixture to the bowl of a food processor. Puree the mixture and then pass through fine sieve. It will be necessary to press down on the mixture in the sieve to press the pulp through, but don't force the raspberry seeds through the sieve.

Return juice to the saucepan; add sugar and bring to a boil. Reduce heat; boil for 5–10 minutes and let cool. Add the Cassis and store in the refrigerator until ready to serve.

To serve, pour 1–2 tablespoons of the syrup into a champagne glass and fill with champagne. It is also nice to put some orange juice with the syrup and then top with champagne.

NOTE: This will keep for weeks.

YIELD: 4 cups of syrup

Sangria Blanca

3½ cups dry
    white wine
½ cup Cointreau
¼ cup sugar
1 (10 oz.) bottle
    club soda or
    1 bottle
    champagne,
    chilled
1 orange, sliced
1 lemon, sliced
1 lime, sliced

   In a punch bowl, combine wine, Cointreau, and sugar. Stir until sugar is dissolved.

Add club soda or champagne just before serving. Garnish with fruit slices.

YIELD: 6 (8-ounce) servings

Southern Comfort Slush

1 (12 oz.) can
    frozen lemonade
1 (6 oz.) can frozen
    orange juice
6 cups water
2 cups brewed tea
1½ cups Southern
    Comfort
1 cup sugar, optional

   Mix all ingredients and place in freezer for 6–8 hours, stirring occasionally to make it a slush.

YIELD: 15 (6-ounce) servings

Hot Apricot Brandy

1 qt. apple juice
½ cup apricot brandy
¼ cup brown sugar
6 whole cloves
6 whole allspice
2 cinnamon sticks

  Mix all ingredients together in a large pot and simmer for 20 minutes.

Strain mixture and pour into mugs. Serve hot.

NOTE: Brandy may be kept in refrigerator and reheated for later use.

YIELD: 6 (8-ounce) servings

Burgundy Apple Punch

2 (1.5 liter) bottles red or rosé wine, chilled
1 qt. apple juice, chilled
2 Tbsp. lemon juice
⅔ cup sugar
1 qt. ginger ale, chilled
Ice ring

In a punch bowl, combine wine, apple juice, lemon juice, and sugar. Stir to dissolve sugar.

When ready to serve, add ginger ale and ice ring; serve at once.

YIELD: 1½ gallons or 48 (4-ounce) servings

Hot Spiced Percolator Punch

1 (46 oz.) can unsweetened pineapple juice

2 (32 oz.) bottles cranberry juice

2 cups water

1 cup brown sugar, packed

10 whole cloves

10 whole allspice

1 12-inch cinnamon stick, broken

Peel of ¼ orange, cut into strips

3 cups light rum, optional

Combine juices with water and brown sugar in a 24-cup percolator. Place cloves, allspice, cinnamon stick pieces, and orange strips in percolator basket.

After punch has perked, rum may be added either to the entire recipe or to individual servings, as desired.

YIELD: 25 servings

Holiday Wassail

1 gallon apple cider
1 cup light brown sugar
1 (6 oz.) can frozen lemonade
1 (6 oz.) can frozen orange juice
12 whole cloves
6 whole allspice
1 tsp. ground nutmeg
1 (4-inch) cinnamon stick
Port wine, optional

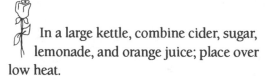 In a large kettle, combine cider, sugar, lemonade, and orange juice; place over low heat.

Tie cloves and allspice into small cloth and add to cider.

Add nutmeg and cinnamon stick; simmer gently for 20 minutes. Add wine, if desired, and heat. Remove from heat and discard spice bag. Serve wassail hot.

YIELD: 4½ quarts or 36 (4-ounce) servings

Queen City Cheese Dip

1 (8 oz.) pkg. cream cheese, softened

8 oz. Cheddar cheese, grated

3 green onions, finely chopped

1 cup mayonnaise

1 tsp. prepared mustard

1 tsp. Salad Supreme

1 tsp. Worcestershire sauce

Dash Tabasco

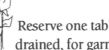 In a large bowl, combine cheeses, onions, mayonnaise, mustard, Salad Supreme, Worcestershire sauce, and Tabasco sauce. Mix until well-blended. Sprinkle additional Salad Supreme over top for garnish.

Serve with favorite crackers or vegetable dippers.

NOTE: Great to use over baked potatoes or spread on English muffins.

YIELD: 3 cups

Spicy Dip Olé

1 (10 oz.) can Rotel tomatoes & green chiles, diced

1 15 oz. can chili (without beans)

1½ cups processed cheese (Velveeta), cubed

½ cup green onions, sliced

½ tsp. cayenne pepper

Ripe olives, sliced

Reserve one tablespoon Rotel tomatoes, drained, for garnish.

In a saucepan, combine all ingredients. Heat just until cheese melts, stirring frequently.

Garnish dip with reserved tomatoes, red pepper, and additional green onion, if desired. Sliced ripe olives may be used for contrast.

NOTE: Serve warm with assorted raw vegetable dippers, toasted french bread slices, tortilla chips, or other chips.

YIELD: 2 cups

Southwest Artichoke Dip

1 (4 oz.) jar
  pimientos, diced
1 (14 oz.) can
  artichoke hearts,
  drained, chopped
1½ cups mayonnaise
2 (7 oz.) cans green
  chiles, drained,
  diced
4 oz. Monterey Jack
  cheese, shredded
½ cup Parmesan
  cheese, grated
Additional
  Parmesan cheese,
  grated
Corn chips or
  tortilla chips

 Drain pimientos and reserve 2 teaspoons for garnish.

In a medium bowl, mix pimientos, artichokes, mayonnaise, green chiles, Monterey Jack cheese, and ½ cup Parmesan cheese. Spread mixture into a shallow 1½-quart baking dish. Sprinkle with additional Parmesan cheese and 2 teaspoons of pimientos. This can be made ahead. Cover and refrigerate.

Bake uncovered at 325° for 30 minutes until bubbly. Serve with corn chips or tortilla chips.

NOTE: May add two 6 oz. packages of frozen crabmeat.

YIELD: 20 appetizer servings

Leaning Tower Pizza Dip

½ cup mayonnaise

1 clove garlic

1 tsp. basil, leaf

½ cup lemon juice

¼ tsp. dried red pepper flakes

8 oz. cream cheese, softened

8 oz. seafood cocktail sauce

1 can baby shrimp, drained

6 oz. black olives, chopped

½ cup onion, chopped

½ cup green pepper, chopped

1 cup celery, finely chopped

¼ lb. pepperoni, chopped

1 cup Mozzarella cheese, grated

1 cup Cheddar cheese, grated

In a blender, mix the first 5 ingredients. Add cream cheese to mixture and spread on serving platter or 9x13-inch casserole. Pour seafood cocktail sauce over the base mixture, then layer the next 6 ingredients.

Combine the two grated cheeses and cover the top of dip. Serve with king-size corn chips.

SERVES: 10 – 12

Sesame Chicken Bites With Honey Dip

1½ cups mayonnaise, divided

1 tsp. dry mustard

1 tsp. onion, minced

½ cup bread crumbs

¼ cup sesame seeds

2 cups cooked chicken, cut into 1½-inch cubes

2 Tbsp. honey

In a mixing bowl, combine ½ cup mayonnaise, mustard, and onion. In a separate bowl, mix bread crumbs and sesame seeds.

Coat cooked chicken with mayonnaise mixture, then bread crumbs.

Bake at 425° for 12 minutes.

Prepare dip by mixing remaining 1 cup mayonnaise and honey.

YIELD: Approximately 4½ cups

Tomato Rose Guacamole

1 medium tomato

2 very ripe, medium avocados, mashed

½ cup onion, finely chopped

2 Tbsp. green chiles, chopped

1 Tbsp. lime juice

1 tsp. salt

½ tsp. pepper

½ tsp. Fruit Fresh

1 tsp. coriander leaves, chopped

Peel tomato in one continuous spiral; save for garnish. Cut tomato in half and squeeze each half to remove juice and seeds; chop.

Mix next 8 ingredients. Stir in chopped tomato. Curl tomato peel around to form a rose and place on top of guacamole. Use extra coriander leaves to finish off the garnish.

YIELD: Approximately 1½ cups

Stuffed Eggplant Dip

1 large eggplant,
  reserve shell
  for bowl

1 Tbsp. lemon juice

¼ cup olive oil or
  vegetable oil

1 green pepper,
  seeded, diced

2 celery stalks, diced

½ cup onion, diced

1 carrot, finely
  chopped

1 garlic clove,
  crushed

1 Tbsp. red wine
  vinegar

2 tomatoes, peeled,
  seeded, and
  chopped

2 Tbsp. cilantro
  leaves, chopped

¼ tsp. dried basil
  leaves

1 tsp. salt

⅛ tsp. cayenne pepper
  Pita bread or
  sourdough bread

Cut eggplant in half lengthwise. Use a spoon to scoop out pulp, leaving a ½-inch shell; reserve pulp.

Brush inside of eggplant shells with lemon juice to prevent browning; set aside for use as a serving container for the vegetable dip.

In a medium saucepan, steam or cook reserved pulp in boiling water until tender, about 8 minutes; set aside.

In a large skillet, heat oil. Add green pepper, celery, onion, and carrot. Sauté until vegetables are tender, 3–4 minutes. Stir in garlic, vinegar, tomatoes, cilantro, basil, salt, cayenne pepper, and cooked eggplant pulp. Stirring occasionally, cook over medium heat 10–15 minutes or until vegetables are very tender.

Cut pita or sourdough bread into wedges; set aside.

Spoon cooked vegetable mixture into eggplant shells. Serve warm or refrigerate 1 hour and serve as a dip with pita or sourdough bread.

YIELD: 3½ cups

Piña Colada Fruit Dip

1 (8 oz.) can
   crushed pineapple
   in its own juice,
   undrained
1 (3½ oz.) pkg.
   instant coconut
   pudding and pie
   filling mix
¾ cup milk
½ cup dairy
   sour cream

In food processor bowl with metal blade or electric blender, combine all ingredients. Cover; process 30 seconds. If using blender, stir after 15 seconds.

Refrigerate several hours or overnight to blend flavors.

Place dip in a pineapple boat and serve with variety of fresh fruits.

YIELD: 2½ cups

Pineapple Dip

⅓ cup sugar
4 Tbsp. cornstarch
¼ tsp. salt
3 Tbsp. lemon juice
1 cup unsweetened
   pineapple juice
2 eggs, beaten
6 oz. cream cheese,
   softened

In a heavy saucepan, combine dry ingredients. Blend in the fruit juices. Cook 5–8 minutes, stirring constantly until clear.

Slowly stir in the eggs. Return to heat and cook over low heat, stirring constantly, 3–4 minutes or until thickened slightly.

Cool 5 minutes and beat in softened cream cheese.

NOTE: This makes a good dip for fresh fruit in slices or chunks. May also be used as a fruit filling for tea sandwiches if you use crushed pineapple (8 ounces) instead of the juice.

YIELD: 2 cups

Shrimp à la Greque

¼ lb. sun dried
    tomatoes
2 cloves garlic, finely
    chopped
3 Tbsp. capers,
    drained
½ tsp. oregano
2 lbs. raw shrimp,
    peeled, deveined
2 cups Feta cheese,
    crumbled
2 Tbsp. olive oil

 Boil tomatoes for 2 minutes in 2 quarts of water. Drain and chop coarsely.

Combine all ingredients and refrigerate for several hours or overnight.

Place in shallow baking dish or individual baking dishes.

Bake at 450° for 10 minutes.

NOTE: May top with Feta cheese just before baking instead of combining with other ingredients.

SERVES: 8

Swiss Cheese Fondue

24 oz. Swiss cheese,
    cubed
12 oz. Muenster
    cheese, cubed
6 oz. Monterey Jack
    cheese, cubed
2 Tbsp. flour
1 clove garlic, halved
1⅛ cups dry
    white wine
⅛ tsp. nutmeg
⅛ tsp. ground white
    pepper
3 Tbsp. kirshwasser

In a small bowl, coat cubed cheese with flour; set aside. Pour wine into a heavy pan that has had the bottom and sides rubbed with garlic. Warm wine until bubbles start to rise (do not boil or cover).

Add cheese a handful at a time, stirring constantly until all has been added and melted.

Add seasonings and kirshwasser when melted cheese starts to bubble.

Serve with cubed bread.

YIELD: 3 cups

Spinach Artichoke Soufflé

2 (10 oz.) pkg. frozen spinach, chopped

1 (14 oz.) can artichoke hearts

½ cup plus 2 Tbsp. butter, divided

½ cup onion, finely chopped

4 oz. cream cheese, softened

⅔ cup Mozzarella cheese, shredded

1¼ cups Parmesan cheese, grated, divided

½ cup heavy cream

2 tsp. lemon juice

½ tsp. pepper

4 drops Tabasco

 Cook the spinach according to package directions and drain well.

Rinse the artichokes with water. Drain, then chop coarsely.

Sauté the onions in 2 tablespoons butter until transparent; set aside.

Mix the cream cheese with remaining ½ cup melted butter and combine with the spinach and artichokes. Add the Mozzarella cheese, 1 cup Parmesan cheese, heavy cream, lemon juice, sautéed onion, pepper, and Tabasco; mix well.

Bake at 350° for 30 minutes. During the last 15 minutes, top with remaining grated Parmesan cheese.

NOTE: This can be served as an appetizer dip or as a vegetable accompaniment.

• May use 20 ounces of fresh spinach, chopped, cooked, and drained.

SERVES: 6–8

Caviar Pie

1 (3–4 oz.) jar
  black lumpfish or
  whitefish caviar

6 eggs, hard-cooked

⅓ cup butter
  or margarine,
  softened

2 tsp. Dijon mustard

2 tsp. white
  wine vinegar

1 tsp. fresh dill,
  chopped, or 1 tsp.
  dill weed

1 cup green onions,
  including tops,
  chopped

3 Tbsp. pimientos,
  chopped, drained

1 (8 oz.) pkg. cream
  cheese, softened

⅔ cup sour cream

  Dill sprigs

  Lemon, thinly
  sliced

  Unsalted crackers

Empty caviar into a fine wire strainer and rinse with cold water; let drain. Cover and refrigerate.

Combine eggs, butter, mustard, vinegar, and dill in food processor or blender until smooth. Salt to taste. Spread in a 9-inch tart pan with a removable bottom. Top with green onions and pimientos. Cover and refrigerate until firm, about 1 hour.

Blend cream cheese and sour cream until smooth. Spoon about two-thirds of the mixture over green onions and pimientos. Using a pastry tube with a star tip, pipe remaining cream cheese mixture decoratively around edge. Cover loosely and refrigerate for at least 1 hour. Pie may be made as early as 1 day in advance.

Just before serving, remove sides of pan and spoon caviar into center of pie. Decorate with dill sprigs and lemon slices. Cut into thin wedges to serve with crackers.

SERVES: 12–16

Chicken Nut Paté

1 cup pecan halves

1 cup walnut halves

1 lb. boneless, skinless chicken breast halves, cooked

2 cloves garlic

1 cup mayonnaise

2 Tbsp. crystallized ginger, minced

1 Tbsp. soy sauce

2 tsp. Worcestershire sauce

1 tsp. white wine vinegar

½ cup green onion, minced

In a food processor bowl with chopping blade, combine pecans and walnuts. Process until coarsely ground. Set aside.

Cut chicken into cubes. Chop chicken and garlic in food processor until very fine.

Add mayonnaise, ginger, soy sauce, Worcestershire sauce, and vinegar. Process by cycling on and off until well-processed. Stir in green onion and nuts.

Spoon mixture into crock. Chill thoroughly, preferably overnight.

NOTE: Serve with crackers or bread sticks. This will keep 2–3 weeks in refrigerator and freezes well.

YIELD: 1 quart

Veal and Ham Paté

5 cloves garlic
2 Tbsp. butter
1 cup onion, chopped
¼ cup brandy or
    Madeira
1 lb. lean
    ground veal
1 lb. lean
    ground pork
¼ tsp. ground cloves
¼ tsp. allspice
¼ tsp. nutmeg
2 eggs
2 tsp. salt
1½ tsp. sage
1½ tsp. pepper
1 tsp. thyme
½ lb. ham, cut in
    strips (cured but
    uncooked)
3 bay leaves
6 strips bacon

 Using metal blade in food processor, drop garlic cloves through feed tube and mince.

Heat butter in a medium-size skillet; add onions and sauté until tender. Place onions and remaining ingredients, except ham, bay leaves, and bacon, in the food processor to make paté. Process until smooth and well-blended.

Spray one large or two medium-size bread pans with vegetable spray. Place a layer of meat mixture on the bottom of the pan; arrange half of the ham strips on top; add another layer of meat mixture, rest of ham strips, and finish with the remaining paté. Place bay leaves on the top. Place bacon strips over the surface.

Cover pan with foil and place it in a larger pan. Pour very hot water into the larger pan, to a depth of at least 1 inch.

Bake at 350° for 1 hour. Remove foil from top of paté. Bake additional 30 minutes. Lift out baking pan and let cool until lukewarm. If there are a lot of juices, pour off about half.

Place clean foil on top of paté and add heavy weights such as cans of food, pie weights, etc. Place paté in refrigerator with weights on top and refrigerate for at least 1 day. When ready to serve, remove weights and foil; unmold and slice.

NOTE: Best prepared 2 days ahead. Freezes well.

SERVES: 8

Crabmeat and Shrimp Mold

1 can crabmeat,
   flaked
1 can broken shrimp
1 can cream of
   mushroom soup
2 envelopes
   unflavored gelatin
¼ cup cold water
8 oz. cream cheese
2 tsp. chili sauce
1 tsp. lemon juice
1 cup mayonnaise
1 cup celery, finely
   chopped
½ cup onion, finely
   chopped

 Rinse crabmeat and shrimp under cold water. Drain well and set aside.

Heat soup. Dissolve gelatin in ¼ cup cold water; add to hot soup.

With mixer, mix cream cheese, chili sauce, lemon juice, and mayonnaise. Add to hot soup mixture.

Fold in crabmeat, shrimp, celery, and onion. Pour into oiled mold.

NOTE: Salmon can be substituted for crabmeat and/or shrimp, if desired.

SERVES: 20

Brie en Croûte

1 lb. wedge
  Brie cheese
½ cup blue cheese,
  crumbled
½ cup pecans,
  chopped
½ pkg. frozen phyllo
  dough, thawed
1 egg
1 Tbsp. water

Cut Brie in half, horizontally. Sprinkle the bottom half with blue cheese and pecans; replace top.

Roll dough on lightly floured surface until large enough to enclose cheese. Place in a lightly greased shallow pan; place Brie in center.

Combine egg and 1 tablespoon water. Fold pastry over Brie and seal with egg mixture, seam side down. Trim pastry so it is no more than 2 layers thick in any spot; reserve scraps. Brush pastry with egg mixture. Cut scraps into flower shapes; arrange on top. Brush again with egg mixture. Cover; chill.

When ready to serve, cover and bake at 375° for 25 minutes or until golden. Serve with fruit.

SERVES: 8

Havarti Cheese Pastry

1 tsp. Dijon mustard
12 oz. Havarti cheese
1 tsp. parsley flakes
½ tsp. chives
¼ tsp. dill weed
¼ tsp. basil
¼ tsp. fennel seeds
½ pkg. frozen puff pastry, flat sheets
1 egg, slightly beaten

Spread mustard on top of cheese; sprinkle with seasonings. Roll out dough on lightly floured surface until large enough to enclose cheese. Place cheese, mustard side down, in center of pastry. Fold dough over cheese and seal edges with beaten egg. Trim excess pastry.

Place seam side down on lightly greased baking sheet. Chill 30 minutes.

Bake at 375° for 20 minutes. Brush with egg and bake 10 more minutes or until brown.

SERVES: 6–8

Cheese Bars

2 (5 oz.) jars Old
   English sharp
   cheese spread,
   softened
¾ cup margarine,
   softened
1 egg, beaten
   Paprika to taste
1 (16 oz.) loaf very
   thin sandwich
   bread (Pepperidge
   Farms)

Combine softened cheese and margarine; mix until smooth. Add egg, beating until well-mixed.

Cut off crust from bread and slice in half. Spread cheese mixture on bottom half of bread and put other half on top. Spread top and 4 sides with more cheese mixture. Sprinkle top with paprika.

Refrigerate overnight on cookie sheets.

Bake at 350° for 20 minutes.

NOTE: These bars can also be frozen before baking. Place bars on cookie sheets in freezer until frozen, remove with spatula and transfer to a freezer plastic bag until ready to use. Remove as many as needed, using the same baking directions.

• For use as a canape, cut the bars in half again and top with cut slices of tiny cocktail sausages before baking.

YIELD: 16 bars

Cheddar Biscuits

3 cups Cheddar
    cheese, grated
1 cup margarine
2 cups flour
1½ tsp. salt
½ tsp. red pepper

 In a large bowl, combine all ingredients. Pinch off 2-inch balls and flatten on cookie sheet with fingers.

Bake at 350° for 8–10 minutes, until golden.

NOTE: Be careful not to overbake. Can store in an airtight tin container. Good with salad.

YIELD: Approximately 30 balls

Cheese Puffs

1 loaf white
    sandwich bread,
    sliced
½ cup butter, melted
1 (8 oz.) pkg. cream
    cheese, softened
½ cup Parmesan
    cheese
6 green onions,
    including tops,
    minced
12 drops Tabasco
3 Tbsp. mayonnaise

Using a biscuit cutter, cut 2 rounds from each slice of bread to equal 40 rounds.

Melt butter and spread on one side of bread. Under broiler, brown, then turn bread over and brown other side.

Combine cream cheese, Parmesan, onions, Tabasco, and mayonnaise; spread on buttered side.

Broil until bubbly.

YIELD: 40 rounds

Working With Phyllo Dough

Cut the sheets of dough.

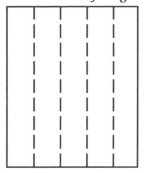

Fold strips in half, place filling on dough and fold like a flag.

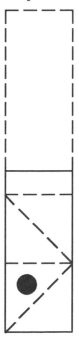

 Phyllo dough is available in the frozen foods section of many grocery stores.

Stack the number of sheets required for the recipe with the short side toward you. Cut the sheets lengthwise into 4–5 strips approximately 3 inches wide.

Because this fragile pastry dries out quickly, work with only 1 strip at a time. Place remaining strips between 2 layers of plastic wrap; cover with a damp cloth.

Remove 1 strip and brush with the oil mixture; sprinkle lightly with fine bread crumbs, about ½ teaspoon. Fold the top half down over the bottom half.

Place 1 teaspoon of desired filling on folded dough, approximately ½ inch from the side and 1½ inches from the bottom (refer to diagram at left). Fold the unfilled corner of pastry over the filling, forming a triangle. Lifting the lower left corner, fold the triangle up; lifting the lower left corner again, fold triangle over to the right. Continue as if folding a flag. Fold any extra pastry under the finished triangle.

Brush the triangles with remaining butter and place, seam side down, on a cookie sheet. Freeze 30 minutes. Bake as directed or transfer triangles to zippered plastic bags and return to freezer for later use.

Swiss Jack Triangles

For the Filling:
½ cup fresh parsley
3 eggs
1 tsp. baking powder
½ lb. Monterey Jack cheese
½ lb. Gruyère
⅓ cup green onion, chopped
1 tsp. caraway seeds

For the Triangles:
½ cup olive oil
½ cup butter
12 phyllo sheets, about ½ lb.
Fine bread crumbs, as needed

FILLING

In a processor bowl fitted with steel blade, chop parsley medium-fine. Add eggs and baking powder; process to blend.

Remove steel blade and fit with medium grating disc; add cheese through feed tube. Remove work bowl from machine; add green onion and caraway seeds. Stir well to combine.

TRIANGLES

In a small pan or dish, melt together olive oil and butter.

To form triangles, follow the directions on page 39, Working With Phyllo Dough.

Completed turnovers may be refrigerated or frozen and baked at your convenience.

Bake at 375° approximately 15–20 minutes, until golden brown and crisp, turning once. If frozen, defrost 30 minutes before baking.

YIELD: 48–60

Curried Chicken Triangles

For the Filling:

2 chicken breasts, boneless and skinless

5 garlic cloves, halved

2 Tbsp. unsalted butter

1 tsp. curry powder

½ cup onion, finely chopped

5 green onions, chopped

⅔ cup white wine

½ cup canned tomato sauce

1 tsp. dried oregano

1 tsp. dried basil

2 tsp. dried rosemary

⅓ cup Parmesan cheese, freshly grated

½ cup fresh parsley, chopped

1 egg, slightly beaten

Pinch of cinnamon

½ tsp. salt

For the Triangles:

½ cup olive oil

½ cup butter

12 phyllo sheets, about ½ lb.

Fine bread crumbs, as needed

FILLING

Dice chicken breasts into 1-inch cubes. Add garlic cloves and, in food processor, blend until smooth.

In a large, heavy-bottomed skillet, over medium heat, melt butter. Add curry powder and both onions; sauté 3–4 minutes.

Stir in processed chicken. Cook until it is no longer pink, stirring constantly.

Add wine, tomato sauce, oregano, basil, and rosemary. Simmer for about 10 minutes. Cool.

Stir in Parmesan, parsley, egg, cinnamon, and salt; set aside.

TRIANGLES

In a small pan or dish, melt together olive oil and butter.

To form triangles, follow the directions on page 39, Working With Phyllo Dough.

Completed turnovers may be refrigerated or frozen and baked at your convenience.

Bake at 375° approximately 15–20 minutes, until golden brown and crisp, turning once. If frozen, defrost 30 minutes before baking.

YIELD: 48–60

Crab Rangoon

1 (8 oz.) pkg. cream cheese

1 (6½ oz.) can crabmeat

1½ tsp. lemon juice, or to taste

1 clove garlic, or to taste

½ pkg. wonton wrappers

1 egg, beaten

Oil to deep fry

Blend cream cheese, crabmeat, lemon juice, and garlic; cover and refrigerate to blend flavors.

Separate wrappers. Place 1 tablespoon crab mixture in center of each wrapper. Brush perimeter of wrapper with beaten egg. Seal edges tightly from points.

Deep fry until golden. Serve immediately.

NOTE: Serve with sweet and sour sauce, hot mustard sauce, or soy sauce.

SERVES: 10–12

Smoked Salmon Pizza

1 (8 oz.) can refrigerated crescent rolls

8 oz. cream cheese, softened

Milk, as needed

Smoked salmon thin filets (available in refrigerated section)

Green onions, thinly sliced using lots of green

Press crescent roll dough onto pizza pan or cookie sheet. Bake at 375° until lightly browned; cool slightly. Spread with cream cheese. If needed, cheese may be thinned with milk for easier spreading. Arrange salmon on cheese layer; top with onions.

Place under broiler at 375° until hot.

NOTE: If broiler setting is only possible at 500°, place on middle shelf and watch to be sure it does not burn.

SERVES: 10

Mushroom Tarts

For the Tart Shells:
⅔ cup butter
2½ cups sifted flour
½ tsp. salt
⅓ cup sour cream
1 egg, beaten

For the Filling:
½ lb. mushrooms, finely chopped
2 Tbsp. green onions, finely chopped
¼ cup butter
¼ cup flour
½ tsp. salt
1 cup heavy cream

TART SHELLS

Cut in ⅔ cup butter, flour, and salt. Add sour cream and egg. Mix with pastry blender. Press dough into small balls and line sides and bottom of miniature muffin cups.

Bake shells at 400° for 12–15 minutes. Cool on racks and remove carefully.

FILLING

Sauté mushrooms and onions in ¼ cup butter. Stir in flour, salt, and heavy cream. Cook, stirring constantly until thick and smooth.

Fill shells with mushroom mixture and serve.

NOTE: Unbaked shells may be stored frozen, then reheated at 400° for 12–15 minutes.

YIELD: 48 tarts

Skinny Party Mix

2 (½ oz.) envelopes
  butter-flavored mix
  (Butter Buds)
¼ cup water
¼ cup Worcestershire
  sauce
2 Tbsp. oil
½ tsp. garlic powder
½ tsp. seasoned salt
  Tabasco,
  several drops
5 cups pretzels
4 cups wheat or bran
  square cereal
3 cups oyster
  crackers
2 cups bite-size
  round crackers

 Coat large roasting pan with vegetable spray.

In a small saucepan, combine butter-flavored mix, water, Worcestershire sauce, oil, garlic powder, salt, and Tabasco. Place over medium heat, stirring until well-blended and heated through.

In a large bowl, combine the pretzels, cereals, and crackers. Pour the butter mixture over all and toss until well-coated.

Pour mixture into prepared pan.

Bake at 300° for 45 minutes, stirring every 15 minutes.

SERVES: 32

Circa 1892, Age 7

Mrs. Truman's Bran Rolls

½ cup sugar
⅔ cup shortening
1 cup all bran
2 teaspoons salt

Pour over this 1 cup boiling water; stir until dissolved and cool.

Add 2 eggs beaten slightly and 2 cakes yeast, dissolved. Add 1 cup warm water and 7 cups white flour.

Put mixture in ice box. Make (into rolls) 2 hours before using. Bake at 400° for 15 to 20 minutes.

TOP: Bess is shown here eating watermelon with family and neighbors in the back yard of the Gates-Wallace home, circa 1904.

ABOVE: Bessie Madge Andrews, a family friend, joined the Wallace children for this 1904 photograph. Left to right: George (holding his dog, Gyp), Fred, Bess and Frank.

Applesauce Rhubarb Muffins

2 cups flour

1 cup whole
   wheat flour

2 tsp. baking powder

4 tsp. cinnamon,
   divided

½ tsp. baking soda

½ tsp. salt

2 eggs

1⅓ cups brown sugar

1⅓ cups applesauce

½ cup oil

1½ cups rhubarb,
   frozen or fresh,
   coarsely chopped

⅓ cup granulated
   sugar

In a large mixing bowl, combine flours, baking powder, 2 teaspoons cinnamon, baking soda, and salt. Make a well in the center; set aside.

In another bowl, mix eggs, brown sugar, applesauce, and oil. Add egg mixture to flour mixture and stir until moistened. Fold in rhubarb.

Fill greased muffin tins two-thirds full. Mix 2 teaspoons cinnamon and granulated sugar. Sprinkle on each muffin. Bake at 400° for 18–20 minutes.

YIELD: 24 muffins

Banana Muffins

2 cups flour
2½ tsp. baking powder
½ tsp. salt
½ cup butter, softened
1 cup plus 1 Tbsp.
   sugar, divided
2 eggs
1 tsp. vanilla
1½ cups very ripe
   banana, mashed
¼ cup milk
½ tsp. cinnamon

 Combine the flour, baking powder, and salt; set aside.

In a large bowl, using an electric mixer, cream the butter and 1 cup of sugar until light and fluffy. Add the eggs one at a time; beat in the vanilla.

Combine the bananas and milk. Stir the flour mixture into the egg mixture alternately with the bananas, stirring until combined. Spoon into greased muffin tin.

Combine remaining 1 tablespoon sugar and cinnamon. Sprinkle over muffins.

Bake at 375° for 30 minutes. Cool in pan 5 minutes.

YIELD: 12 muffins

Morning Glory Muffins

½ cup raisins

2¼ cups all-purpose flour

1 cup sugar

2 tsp. baking soda

1 Tbsp. cinnamon

½ tsp. salt

2 cups carrots, grated

1 large apple, peeled, cored and grated

1 (8 oz.) can crushed pineapple with juice

½ cup almonds, slivered

½ cup shredded coconut

3 eggs

1 cup vegetable oil

2 tsp. vanilla

 Cover raisins with hot water and soak 30 minutes. Drain thoroughly.

Generously grease ½-cup muffin tin, or line with paper baking cups. Mix flour, sugar, baking soda, cinnamon, and salt in bowl. Stir in raisins, carrots, apple, pineapple, almonds, and coconut.

Beat eggs with oil and vanilla to blend. Stir into flour mixture until just combined. Divide batter among muffin cups.

Bake at 350° for 20–22 minutes or until golden brown. Cool 5 minutes before removing from pan. Serve at room temperature.

NOTE: Flavor improves if made 1 day ahead.

YIELD: 15 muffins

Green Chile Cornbread

2 eggs

1¼ cups oil

1 (4 oz.) can green chiles

1 (9 oz.) can cream style corn

½ cup sour cream or plain yogurt

1 cup yellow cornmeal

½ tsp. salt

2 Tbsp. baking powder

2 cups Cheddar cheese, grated, divided

Blend eggs, oil, and chiles. Add corn, sour cream (or yogurt), cornmeal, salt, baking powder, and 1½ cups cheese; blend. Pour into oiled 9-inch square pan and sprinkle remaining cheese on top.

Bake at 350° for 1 hour.

SERVES: 6–8

Sweet Cornbread

1 (18 oz.) pkg.
yellow cake mix

1 (15 oz.) pkg.
cornbread mix

Additional
ingredients as
required on box
directions

Prepare the cake and cornbread mixes according to package directions. Combine the 2 batters and blend well.

Pour into a 9x13-inch oiled baking pan and bake at 350° for 30–35 minutes or until center tests done.

NOTE: May use 1 (9 oz.) package yellow cake mix and 1 (8½ oz.) package cornbread mix. Prepare as above and place in an 8-inch square greased baking pan. Bake as directed above, decreasing baking time to 20 minutes or until cake tests done.

- Great served with honey butter.

- Serve with chili.

SERVES: 12

Chive Muffins

2 cups all-purpose
flour

1 Tbsp. baking
powder

¼ cup dried chives

1 Tbsp. granulated
sugar

1 Tbsp. brown sugar

1 egg, slightly beaten

1 cup milk

¼ cup butter, melted

Combine first 5 ingredients in a large bowl; make a well in center of mixture. Combine egg, milk, and butter; add to dry ingredients, stirring just until moistened.

Spoon batter into greased muffin pans, filling two-thirds full.

Bake at 400° for 18–20 minutes or until lightly browned. Remove from pans immediately.

YIELD: 12 muffins

Herbed French Bread

1 long loaf French
  bread
½ lb. butter
1 cup parsley,
  chopped
¼ cup green onions,
  chopped
¼ cup chives,
  chopped, optional
2 cloves garlic,
  crushed

 Split French loaf lengthwise. Combine all ingredients and spread on French loaf halves.

Wrap in double thickness of aluminum foil. Heat on grill or in oven until warm. Slice and serve warm.

SERVES: 12–16

Bread Sticks

1 pkg. hot dog buns
¾ cup margarine,
  melted
  Garlic salt to taste
  Dry salad
  seasonings to taste

 Slice each bun into 6–8 strips; place on large baking sheet.

Spread half of margarine on buns. Sprinkle lightly with garlic and seasoning. Turn bread over and repeat.

Bake at 225° for 2½ hours; turn once. Store in airtight container up to two weeks.

YIELD: 4–5 dozen

Cinnamon Roll-Ups

2 loaves sandwich
   bread
16 oz. cream cheese,
   softened
½ tsp. lemon juice
1½ cups sugar, divided
2 egg yolks
1 cup margarine,
   melted
2 Tbsp. cinnamon

Cut off crusts from bread and flatten until thin, using rolling pin. Cream together cream cheese, lemon juice, ½ cup sugar, and egg yolks; spread over bread. Roll the bread like a jelly roll.

Mix remaining sugar and cinnamon together. Dip rolled bread in the melted margarine; roll in the sugar and cinnamon mixture.

Slice each roll in half. Place in greased pan to freeze. You can also freeze in zippered plastic bags.

Bake at 450° for 10 minutes, longer if frozen.

NOTE: Serve for breakfast, brunch, or snack.

YIELD: 20–40 roll-ups

English Muffin Bread

6 cups flour, divided;
  sift before
  measuring
2 pkgs. dry yeast
1 Tbsp. sugar
2 tsp. salt
¼ tsp. baking soda
2 cups milk
½ cup water
⅓ cup corn meal,
  divided

 In a large mixing bowl, combine 3 cups flour, dry yeast, sugar, salt, and soda.

In a saucepan, combine milk and water; heat to 125°. Add to dry mixture; beat with wooden spoon. Stir in remaining flour. Batter will be stiff.

Oil two 8½x4½-inch loaf pans and sprinkle sides and bottom with ¼ cup corn meal. Spoon batter into prepared pans and sprinkle top with remaining corn meal.

Cover with wax paper and let rise for 45 minutes.

Bake at 375° for 25 minutes. Remove from pan immediately and cool.

NOTE: This bread freezes well.

YIELD: 2 loaves

Cornmeal Roll

2 cups milk
⅓ cup cornmeal
⅓ cup sugar
1 tsp. salt
½ cup butter
1 pkg. yeast
¼ cup warm water
  (110°–115°)
2 eggs
5½ cups flour

In a saucepan, combine milk, cornmeal, sugar, salt, and butter. Cook over medium heat, stirring until thick. Remove from heat. Cool to lukewarm.

Soften yeast in water. Add yeast, eggs, and flour to cooled mixture until it forms a soft dough.

Knead lightly until smooth. Let rise until double in bulk. Punch down, let rise once more; punch down again and form into desired shapes.

Bake at 350° for 20–30 minutes or until browned.

NOTE: This dough may be rolled out, cut with biscuit cutter, or formed into any shape desired.

YIELD: 3–4 dozen

Refrigerator Parkerhouse Rolls

1 pkg. dry yeast
1 cup warm water
   (110°–115°)
1 cup shortening
¾ cup sugar
1 Tbsp. salt
1 cup boiling water
2 eggs, well-beaten
6¼ cups flour
   Additional butter,
   melted

 Soften yeast in water; set aside.

Cream shortening, sugar, and salt. Add boiling water and cool to lukewarm. Add eggs, softened yeast, and flour; mix well.

Place in refrigerator at least 2 hours (overnight is better). Roll out dough on lightly floured board.

Cut into rounds with floured 2-inch biscuit cutter.

Make crease with back of knife across each round, just off-center. Brush smaller half with butter and fold over large half.

Place rolls close together on greased baking sheet; cover. Let rise 1½–2 hours.

Bake at 425° about 15 minutes.

YIELD: 5–6 dozen

Orange Rolls

For the Rolls:

1 pkg. dry yeast

¼ cup warm water (110°–115°)

½ cup sour cream

¾ cup sugar, divided

1 tsp. salt

½ cup butter, melted, divided

2 eggs, beaten

3½ cups all-purpose flour, divided

3 Tbsp. orange rind, grated

For the Glaze:

¼ cup sugar

¼ cup sour cream

2 Tbsp. butter

1 Tbsp. orange juice

 ROLLS

Dissolve yeast in warm water; let stand 5 minutes.

Combine sour cream, ¼ cup sugar, and salt in a bowl; mix well. Add 6 tablespoons melted butter, eggs, 2 cups flour, and yeast mixture; mix well. Add enough remaining flour to make soft dough.

Turn dough out on a floured surface and knead until smooth and elastic, about 5 minutes. Place in a well-greased bowl, turning to grease top. Cover and let rise in a warm place, free from drafts, 1½–2 hours or until double in bulk. While dough is rising, combine remaining ½ cup sugar and orange rind; set aside.

Punch dough down and divide in half. On a floured surface, roll each half into a 12-inch circle. Brush each circle with 1 tablespoon butter; sprinkle with sugar and orange mixture. Cut into 12 wedges. Roll up each wedge tightly; place point side down on greased baking sheets.

Cover and let rise in a warm place 1 hour or until almost double in bulk. Bake at 350° for 18–20 minutes or until golden. Drizzle orange glaze over hot rolls; remove immediately from pans.

YIELD: 2 dozen rolls

GLAZE

Combine all ingredients in a small pan; mix well. Bring to a boil and cook 3 minutes, stirring constantly.

YIELD: ½ cup

Light Wheat Rolls

2 pkgs. dry yeast
1¾ cups warm water
(110°–115°)
½ cup sugar
1 tsp. salt
¼ cup butter, melted
1 egg, slightly beaten
2¼ cups whole wheat
flour
2¾ cups all-purpose
flour
Additional butter,
melted

In a large bowl, dissolve yeast in warm water. Add sugar and salt to the yeast mixture.

Melt ¼ cup butter; cool to lukewarm. Add butter, egg, and whole wheat flour to yeast mixture, stirring well. Gradually stir in enough flour to make a soft dough. Knead until smooth, about 5 minutes. Place in greased bowl. Turn to coat all sides. Cover and let rise in warm place, 1 hour or until doubled in bulk. Punch down dough; cover and let rise once more.

Punch down dough and divide into equal portions. Roll each portion into a 14x6-inch rectangle. Cut dough into 12 (7x1-inch) strips. Roll each strip into a spiral; place in oiled muffin pans. Brush with melted butter; let rise uncovered in warm place, 40 minutes or until double in bulk. Buttering will prevent rolls from drying out as they rise.

Bake at 400° for 12–15 minutes; brush again with melted butter.

NOTE: Rolls may be prepared ahead of time and frozen. Bake at 400° for 8 minutes; let cool and freeze. Let rolls thaw and bake at 400° for 5–7 minutes.

YIELD: 2 dozen rolls

Egg Rolls

1 cup milk, scalded
½ cup sugar
½ cup shortening,
   softened
1 tsp. salt
3 eggs, beaten
1 pkg. dry yeast
4½ cups flour, sifted
   Additional butter,
   melted

In a saucepan, bring milk to a boil. Remove from heat and add sugar, shortening, and salt. Cool slightly. Add eggs and yeast to the mixture. Stir in sifted flour gradually, until well-mixed.

Cover and let rise until double in bulk. Punch down and place in refrigerator overnight or until thoroughly chilled.

When ready to bake, punch down dough and form into desired shapes; let rise until double in bulk. Bake at 375° for 8–10 minutes. Brush with butter.

YIELD: 2 dozen rolls

Shepherd's Bread

2 cups milk
2 cups water
2 pkgs. dry yeast
4 tsp. salt
6 Tbsp. sugar
4 Tbsp. shortening
5 cups whole wheat flour
6 cups all-purpose or bread flour
Additional butter, melted

In saucepan, combine milk and water; scald. Measure 1 cup hot milk mixture into small bowl; cool to 110°–115°. Add yeast; let bubble for 10 minutes. To remaining liquid, add salt and sugar. Let stand until lukewarm. Add shortening and yeast mixture. Combine thoroughly.

Place milk and yeast mixture in large electric mixer bowl. Using regular beaters, add whole wheat flour 1 cup at a time. Continue beating, adding white flour gradually. When dough becomes stiff, change to dough hook(s) and continue adding flour until dough comes away from sides of bowl. Continue kneading dough with mixer until dough is smooth and elastic. If your mixer does not have dough hooks, continue adding flour until a soft dough is formed. Turn dough onto a lightly floured surface; knead until smooth and elastic, about 5–10 minutes. Add flour only as needed.

Place dough in lightly greased mixing bowl; cover. Let rise at room temperature until double in bulk.

Punch down and turn out on lightly floured surface. Divide into 4 equal pieces and form each into a ball. Grease 9-inch pie plates, cake pans, or baking sheet. Place one piece of dough in pans or 2 balls of dough side by side on baking sheet; cover. Let stand until double in bulk.

Bake at 425° for 15 minutes. Reduce heat to 375°; bake 35 minutes longer. Remove from pans. Brush with melted butter. Cool on racks, uncovered.

YIELD: 4 loaves

Sicilian Flat Bread

1 pkg. dry yeast
1 cup warm water
 (110°–115°)
2 Tbsp. sugar
1 tsp. salt
3½ cups flour
 Olive oil
1 tsp. coarse salt
 for topping

Optional Toppings:

1 small onion,
 thinly sliced
¾ cup Parmesan
 cheese, grated
3 Tbsp. bacon, cooked
 and crumbled
1 Tbsp. sesame seed
 or poppy seed
 Light dusting of
 garlic powder,
 sweet basil, and/or
 oregano

 In a large bowl, dissolve yeast in warm water. Stir in sugar and salt until dissolved.

Gradually add flour, stirring with a spoon until dough can be easily kneaded. Knead on floured surface 5 minutes.

Place dough in an oiled bowl, turning to coat all sides. Cover and let rise 1 hour. Punch down dough and let rise again.

Spread dough thinly on a baking sheet brushed with olive oil. Pierce top of dough with fork; brush with olive oil. Sprinkle with coarse salt and any other desired toppings.

Bake at 450° for 10–15 minutes or until lightly browned.

Tear into individual portions; serve warm.

SERVES: 10–12

Brunch Bread

1 pkg. dry yeast
¼ cup warm water (110°–115°)
3 Tbsp. sugar
½ cup whole milk
1 tsp. salt
1 tsp. whole rosemary
1 egg
¼ cup olive oil
3 cups flour
½ cup white raisins
Additional flour, as needed

 Dissolve yeast in warm water and sugar.

In a saucepan, combine milk, salt, and rosemary. Heat to warm, approximately 110°.

In a large bowl, combine egg with olive oil. Add milk mixture and dissolved yeast. Stir and mix well. Add flour, 1 cup at a time.

Turn dough out onto a floured board and knead for 5 minutes, adding in the raisins as you knead.

Oil a large bowl with additional olive oil. Place dough in this bowl and invert so top surface is oiled.

Cover dough and let rise in a warm place until double in bulk, about 1–1½ hours.

Knead dough again and place on baking sheet coated with olive oil. Pat into a flat round. Brush generously with more olive oil. Cover lightly with plastic wrap or a thin cloth.

Let rise until double in bulk. Slash an "X" across the top of the loaf.

Bake at 350° for 35 minutes or until browned.

SERVES: 12

Marbled Apricot Bread

For the Bread:

- 1 cup dried apricots, cut into thin strips
- ½ cup golden raisins
- 4 Tbsp. butter, softened
- ½ cup granulated sugar
- ½ cup packed light brown sugar
- 1 large egg, room temperature
- 2 cups flour
- 2 tsp. baking powder
- ½ tsp. baking soda
- ½ tsp. salt
- ¾ cup orange juice
- ½ cup walnuts, chopped

For the Filling:

- 6 oz. cream cheese, softened
- ⅓ cup sugar
- 1 large egg, room temperature
- 1 Tbsp. orange rind, grated

BREAD

In a small bowl, combine apricots and raisins. Add boiling water to cover. Let stand 30 minutes; drain. In bowl, beat butter and sugars until creamy. Beat in egg; set aside.

Sift flour, baking powder, baking soda, and salt together. Add flour mixture alternately with orange juice to butter mixture. Stir in apricots, raisins, and walnuts.

FILLING

For the filling, place all ingredients in food processor and process until smooth.

Pour two-thirds of batter into greased and floured 9x5-inch loaf pan. Top with filling, then batter. Insert knife; swirl to marbleize. Bake at 350° for 55–60 minutes or until golden. Cool 10 minutes then turn on to wire rack.

NOTE: May refrigerate dough 1 week or freeze up to 2 months.

YIELD: 1 loaf

Peach Coffee Cake

1 (18½ oz.) pkg.
  yellow cake mix
1 (20 oz.) can peach
  pie filling
3 eggs
1 tsp. lemon extract,
  divided
½ cup nuts, chopped
½ cup sugar
½ cup flour
¼ cup butter, softened

Combine cake mix, pie filling, eggs, ½ teaspoon lemon extract, and nuts. Reserve remaining lemon extract for topping. Using mixer, blend on low until ingredients are moistened, then blend on medium speed for 2 minutes.

Pour batter into a greased and floured 9x13-inch pan.

Combine sugar, flour, butter, and remaining ½ teaspoon lemon extract with a pastry blender. Sprinkle topping over batter in pan.

Bake at 350° for 35–40 minutes.

NOTE: Can serve with whipped cream or use as a short cake with fresh peaches.

SERVES: 16–20

Cherry Coffee Cake

1¼ sticks butter,
   softened, divided
1¼ cups sugar, divided
2 eggs
1 cup sour cream
1 tsp. vanilla
½ tsp. almond extract
2½ cups flour, divided
1½ tsp. baking powder
½ tsp. baking soda
½ tsp. salt
1 can cherry pie
   filling
1 tsp. cinnamon
½ cup nuts, chopped

In a large bowl, cream 1 stick butter and 1 cup sugar. Add eggs, beating well. Mix in sour cream, vanilla, and almond extract.

Sift together 2 cups flour, baking powder, baking soda, and salt; add to creamed mixture.

Spread half of mixture in greased 9x13-inch pan. Cover with cherry pie filling. Spread remaining batter on top.

Combine 2 tablespoons butter, ½ cup flour, ¼ cup sugar, cinnamon, and nuts; sprinkle on top of cake mixture.

Bake at 350° for 45 minutes.

SERVES: 12

Butterscotch Coffee Cake

1 (18½ oz.) pkg.
   yellow cake mix
1 (17½ oz.) can
   prepared
   butterscotch
   pudding
2 eggs
⅓ cup sugar
1 (6 oz.) pkg.
   butterscotch
   morsels
½ cup pecans,
   chopped

In a large mixing bowl, combine cake mix, pudding, and eggs. Mix until well-blended. Pour into greased 9x13-inch pan.

Combine sugar, butterscotch morsels, and pecans. Sprinkle on cake.

Bake at 350° for 35–40 minutes.

NOTE: Delicious for breakfast or brunch; also makes nice dessert.

SERVES: 12

Cranberry Yogurt Coffee Cake

1 (18½ oz.) pkg. yellow cake mix

1 (3¾ oz.) pkg. vanilla instant pudding mix

4 eggs

1 cup unflavored yogurt

¼ cup vegetable oil

1 (16 oz.) can whole berry cranberry sauce

½ cup nuts, chopped

In a large bowl, blend cake mix, pudding mix, eggs, yogurt, and oil. Beat with electric mixer on high for 3 minutes. Scrape bowl often.

Spread two-thirds of batter in a greased and floured 9x13-inch pan. Spoon cranberry sauce evenly over it. Spoon remaining batter evenly over cranberry sauce. Sprinkle with chopped nuts.

Bake at 350° for 55–60 minutes. Cool on rack for 35 minutes.

NOTE: This can be baked in a 12x17-inch jelly roll pan for 30 minutes.

SERVES: 20

Overnight Coffee Cake

2 cups flour
1 tsp. baking powder
1 tsp. baking soda
½ tsp. salt
1½ tsp. cinnamon, divided
⅔ cup margarine, softened
1 cup granulated sugar
1 cup brown sugar, firmly packed, divided
2 eggs
1 cup buttermilk
½ cup walnuts, chopped
¼ tsp. nutmeg

 Sift together flour, baking powder, baking soda, salt, and 1 tsp. cinnamon; set aside.

In a large bowl, combine margarine, 1 cup granulated sugar, and ½ cup brown sugar. Beat until light. Add eggs, 1 at a time, beating well after each addition.

Add flour mixture alternately with buttermilk, starting and ending with flour mixture.

Spread batter in greased 9x13-inch baking pan or 2 round 8-inch pans.

In a small bowl, combine remaining ½ cup brown sugar, walnuts, remaining ½ tsp. cinnamon, and nutmeg. Sprinkle evenly over batter. Cover with plastic wrap and refrigerate overnight.

The next day, remove wrap and bake at 350° for 35–40 minutes until lightly browned and toothpick inserted in center comes out clean.

SERVES: 12

Cream Cheese Coffee Cake

For the Coffee Cake:
2½ cups flour
1 Tbsp. sugar
1 tsp. salt
4 egg yolks
1 cup butter, softened
2 pkgs. dry yeast
¼ cup warm water
(110°–115°)

For the Filling:
2 (8 oz.) pkgs.
cream cheese
1 cup sugar
1 egg yolk

For the Topping:
1 egg white
½ cup nuts, finely
chopped

For the Icing:
1 cup powdered
sugar
2 Tbsp. milk or water

COFFEE CAKE

In a large bowl, combine flour, sugar, salt, egg yolks, and butter. Mix with pastry blender or fork. Dissolve yeast in water. Let stand 3–5 minutes; stir. Add dissolved yeast to flour mixture; mix well. Refrigerate 2 hours.

FILLING

In a separate bowl, mix cheese, sugar, and egg yolk. Beat until smooth.

ASSEMBLY

Divide chilled dough in half. Roll out half the dough and press evenly into lightly oiled 10x15-inch pan. Cover with filling.

Roll remaining dough to 10x15 inches. Place over filling. Pinch edges together.

TOPPING

Beat egg white slightly and brush on top of dough. Sprinkle with nuts. Let rise in warm place 1 hour. Bake at 350° for 30–35 minutes. Let cool slightly.

ICING

Mix powdered sugar with liquid for desired consistency. Drizzle over cooled cake.

SERVES: 20–25

Sausage Ring

1 lb. frozen bread, thawed

1 lb. mild Italian sausage or turkey sausage

2 eggs

½ tsp. Italian seasoning

1½ cups Mozzarella or Monterey Jack cheese, shredded

1 Tbsp. Parmesan cheese, grated

Defrost bread overnight in refrigerator or 2–2½ hours at room temperature. Cook sausage with seasoning until brown; drain and let cool. Add cheese. Beat 1 egg; add to sausage mixture.

Stretch and roll bread into 6x18-inch rectangle. Spoon on meat mixture to within ½ inch of edge. Roll up dough, starting from one of the long sides. Form into a ring and pinch seams to seal. Slash top of ring with knife ½-inch deep and 1½ inches apart.

Beat remaining egg and brush over ring. Sprinkle with Parmesan cheese. Cover and let rise for about 35 minutes until double in bulk. Bake at 350° for 30 minutes or until brown. Serve warm or cool to room temperature.

NOTE: Attractive served with scrambled eggs in center of ring.

• May freeze by wrapping in foil. To serve, defrost completely; cover loosely with foil and bake at 350° for 15 minutes. Uncover and continue heating for 15 minutes.

SERVES: 8–10

Veal Sausage Roll

1 loaf frozen bread
  dough, thawed
2 tsp. margarine
2 tsp. olive oil
1 small garlic clove,
  minced
3 oz. Provolone
  cheese, shredded
3 oz. Mozzarella
  cheese, shredded
10 oz. thinly sliced
  veal sausage,
  cooked and finely
  chopped

Defrost bread dough overnight in refrigerator or 2 – 2½ hours at room temperature.

In small saucepan, heat margarine and oil together over medium heat until mixture is bubbly. Add garlic and sauté until golden, about 1 minute; set aside.

On work surface, press bread dough into a 17x10 inch rectangle. Using pastry brush, place half garlic mixture over the dough. Sprinkle with cheeses and sausage; press firmly into dough.

Starting from wide end, roll dough jelly-roll fashion to enclose filling. Pinch each narrow end to seal and tuck ends beneath loaf.

Transfer loaf, seam-side down, to non-stick baking sheet. Using pastry brush, brush remaining garlic mixture over bread.

Bake at 350° for 30–35 minutes or until golden brown. If bread is browning too quickly, cover with foil. Transfer bread to wire rack and let cool 15 minutes before serving.

SERVES: 16

Italian Frittata

1 lb. sweet Italian
   sausage links

2 Tbsp. olive oil

2 Tbsp. butter

1½ cups red onion,
   chopped

3 garlic cloves, sliced

2 green peppers,
   seeded and cut into
   strips

2 medium potatoes,
   boiled, peeled, and
   diced

2 medium tomatoes,
   peeled and diced

1½ tsp. basil

1½ tsp. oregano

2 Tbsp. parsley,
   minced

   Salt and pepper
   to taste

8 eggs

3 Tbsp. water

½ cup Parmesan
   cheese, grated

 Bring sausage to boil in ½-inch water. Cook 5–10 minutes. Drain and slice sausage ½-inch thick.

Heat oil and butter in 12-inch ovenproof skillet. Sauté onion, garlic, and green pepper until soft. Add sausage slices, potatoes, tomatoes, and herbs; salt and pepper. Mix and sauté for 2 minutes.

Beat eggs lightly with water. Pour over ingredients in skillet. Cook over medium heat until bottom of frittata is set and browned.

Sprinkle with cheese. Broil until top is puffed and browned. Cut into wedges and serve with warm Italian bread.

SERVES: 8

Spinach Quiche

For the Crust:

1 (3 oz.) pkg. cream
   cheese, softened
½ cup butter
1 cup flour

For the Filling:

¾ cup Italian
   sausage, cooked
1 (10 oz.) pkg.
   frozen spinach
   soufflé, thawed
2 eggs, beaten
3 Tbsp. milk
2 tsp. onion, chopped
1 (4 oz.) can
   mushrooms,
   drained
¾ cup Cheddar or
   Swiss cheese,
   grated

CRUST

Combine the cream cheese, butter, and flour; press into a 9-inch pie pan.

FILLING

Remove the casing from Italian sausage; crumble and brown. Drain. Mix remaining ingredients with sausage and pour into pie crust.

Bake at 400° for 25–30 minutes.

SERVES: 4–6

Italian Zucchini Crescent Pie

2 Tbsp. margarine

4 cups zucchini, thinly sliced

1 cup onion, chopped

2 Tbsp. parsley flakes

½ tsp. salt

½ tsp. pepper

¼ tsp. garlic powder

¼ tsp. dried basil, crushed

¼ tsp. dried oregano

2 eggs, well-beaten

1 cup Mozzarella, shredded

1 cup Monterey Jack, shredded

2 Tbsp. pimientos, sliced and drained

1 (8 oz.) can refrigerated crescent rolls

1¼ tsp. prepared mustard

1¼ tsp. Dijon mustard

Melt the margarine in a 10-inch skillet over medium heat. Add the zucchini and onion; cook about 8 minutes or until tender. Stir in the parsley flakes, salt, pepper, garlic powder, basil, and oregano.

Combine the eggs and cheeses in a large bowl; mix well. Add pimientos. Stir in the cooked vegetable mixture; set aside.

Separate the crescent roll dough into 8 triangles. In an ungreased 10-inch pie plate or 11-inch quiche dish, press triangles over the bottom and up the sides to form a crust. Firmly press the perforations together to seal.

Mix the mustards and spread over the crust. Pour egg mixture evenly over mustard.

Bake at 375° for 18–22 minutes or until a knife inserted near the center comes out clean. To prevent excessive browning, cover the crust with foil during the last 10–12 minutes of baking. Let the pie stand 10 minutes before serving.

SERVES: 6–8

Spinach and Sausage Frittata

1 lb. sweet Italian sausages, crumbled

¼ cup olive oil

1 cup onion, chopped

1 (10 oz.) pkg. frozen spinach, thawed and drained

½ lb. mushrooms, sliced

6 eggs

1 cup Parmesan cheese, grated and divided

2 garlic cloves, minced

½ tsp. dried basil

¼ tsp. dried marjoram

Salt and freshly ground pepper

1 cup Mozzarella cheese, grated

Remove casings from sausage and brown in large skillet over medium-high heat; remove and drain well. Pour off drippings from skillet. Add oil and heat. Sauté onion until translucent. Add spinach and mushrooms. Cook 2 minutes. Remove from heat.

Butter 9-inch pie plate. Combine eggs, ¾ cup Parmesan, garlic, and seasonings in medium bowl and mix well. Stir in sausage and vegetables. Turn into pie plate and sprinkle with Mozzarella and remaining Parmesan cheese.

Bake at 350° for 25 minutes, or until set.

SERVES: 6–8

Three-Cheese Ham and Pasta Bake

1 lb. spiral pasta noodles

4 Tbsp. vegetable oil, divided

4 small zucchini, cut into ¼-inch slices

1 lb. fresh mushrooms, sliced

6 green onions, minced

2 cloves garlic, minced

4 cups cooked ham, diced

2 Tbsp. parsley, minced

1 tsp. dry oregano

1 (15 oz.) carton Ricotta cheese

1 (10 oz.) pkg. Mozzarella cheese, grated

1 cup Parmesan cheese, grated

1 cup sour cream

3 eggs

1 tsp. Dijon mustard

½ tsp. salt

½ tsp. pepper

1 cup bread crumbs

3 Tbsp. butter

Butter a 4-quart baking dish. Cook pasta according to package directions; drain. Toss with 2 tablespoons oil in large bowl; reserve.

In a large skillet, sauté zucchini, mushrooms, onions, and garlic in remaining oil until crisp-tender, 3–4 minutes. Remove from heat; add ham, parsley, and oregano. Toss to mix; reserve.

In a mixing bowl, beat Ricotta, Mozzarella, and Parmesan cheeses, sour cream, eggs, mustard, salt, and pepper until smooth and well-blended.

Pour cheese mixture over cooked pasta; toss with wooden spoon to mix. Add vegetable mixture and toss gently to mix.

Transfer mixture to prepared dish. Sprinkle top with bread crumbs; dot with butter. Cover and bake at 350° for 30 minutes, or until bubbly. Uncover and bake about 10 minutes to brown.

SERVES: 8–10

Ham and Eggs Brunch Bake

½ cup onion, chopped

1 Tbsp. margarine

1 cup ham, chopped

1 cup tomato, chopped

2 cups biscuit mix

½ cup cold water

1 cup Cheddar or Swiss cheese, shredded

¼ cup milk

2 eggs

¼ tsp. salt

¼ tsp. pepper

¾ tsp. dried dill weed

2 Tbsp. green onion, chopped

In a small pan, sauté onion in margarine until translucent. Remove from heat; stir in ham and tomato.

Combine biscuit mix and water. With floured hands, pat dough into a greased 9x13-inch baking dish, pressing evenly over bottom and ½-inch up the sides of dish.

Spread ham mixture over dough. Sprinkle with shredded cheese.

Beat milk, eggs, salt, pepper, and dill weed until foamy. Pour egg mixture over cheese layer and sprinkle with green onions.

Bake uncovered at 350° for 30 minutes.

SERVES: 6–8

Egg and Artichoke Casserole

2 (6½ oz.) jars
  marinated
  artichoke hearts

¾ cup green onions,
  chopped

1 clove garlic,
  minced

4 eggs, beaten

2 cups medium
  Cheddar cheese,
  grated

6 soda crackers,
  crushed

 Drain artichokes, reserving marinade. Cut artichokes into thirds.

Sauté onion and garlic in 2 tablespoons of reserved marinade.

Brush artichoke marinade on bottom and sides of 9x9-inch baking dish.

Combine artichokes, onion, and garlic with eggs, cheese, and crackers. Pour into prepared dish.

Bake at 350° for 40 minutes.

SERVES: 6

Chile Cheese Eggs

3 (4 oz.) cans diced
  green chiles

8 oz. Monterey Jack
  cheese, grated

16 oz. Cheddar
  cheese, grated

4 eggs

1 (13 oz.) can
  evaporated milk

2 Tbsp. flour

⅛ tsp. salt

1 cup salsa

Spread chiles on the bottom of a greased 9x13-inch baking dish. Sprinkle grated cheeses evenly over chiles.

Beat eggs, milk, flour, and salt with wire whisk. Pour egg mixture over cheese and chiles.

Bake uncovered at 350° for 30 minutes. Cool 15 minutes before cutting; serve within 30 minutes. Top with salsa just before serving.

SERVES: 8

South-of-the Border Breakfast

1 cup sour cream

1 (10¾ oz.) can cream of mushroom soup

1 (4 oz.) can green chiles, chopped

1 cup chunky salsa

¼ tsp. ground cumin

¼ tsp. ground coriander

1 lb. spicy ground sausage

2 Tbsp. butter

6 eggs, slightly beaten

¼ cup cottage cheese

1 Tbsp. fresh parsley, chopped

¼ cup green onions, finely chopped

12 (8-inch) flour tortillas

1 cup mild Cheddar cheese, grated

1 cup Monterey Jack cheese, grated

In a mixing bowl, whisk together sour cream, soup, green chiles, salsa, cumin, and coriander.

In a large skillet, sauté sausage. Drain on paper towels and crumble.

Wipe out skillet and melt butter. Add eggs and cottage cheese; blend. Add parsley and onions; cook until lightly set. Add 2 tablespoons sour cream mixture and sausage. Remove from heat.

Divide filling and spread on tortillas; roll.

Place a small amount of sour cream mixture in buttered 9x13-inch pan. Arrange tortillas on top in a single layer. Top with remaining sour cream mixture. Cover with cheeses.

Bake at 325° for 30–45 minutes.

SERVES: 6–8

Scrumptious Eggs

¾ lb. fresh or canned
   sliced mushrooms,
   drained
1 cup onion, chopped
¼ cup butter
1 cup ham, cubed
24 oz. Monterey Jack
   cheese, shredded,
   divided
7 eggs, beaten
1¾ cups milk
½ cup flour
1 Tbsp. parsley,
   finely chopped
1 tsp. seasoned salt

 In a skillet, sauté mushrooms and onion in butter; add ham and half of cheese.

Place remaining cheese in bottom of buttered 9x13-inch baking dish; spread mushroom mixture over cheese.

In a large bowl, beat eggs, milk, flour, parsley, and seasoned salt. Pour over mushroom mixture.

Bake at 350° for 45 minutes.

SERVES: 10

Eggs Pierre

10 (½-inch) slices
  sourdough French
  bread, buttered
10 slices ham
10 slices Cheddar
  cheese
10 slices Swiss cheese
18 eggs
⅓ cup cream
  Garlic salt to taste
  Pepper to taste
⅛ tsp. Worcestershire
⅛ tsp. thyme
  Dash cayenne

The day before, arrange buttered French bread in an oiled 10x19-inch baking dish. Layer ham and cheeses on top of bread.

Mix remaining ingredients in bowl and whisk for 2–3 minutes. Pour over layered ham and cheeses. Cover and refrigerate overnight.

Remove from refrigerator 1 hour before baking.

Bake at 375° for 20–25 minutes. Top will be crispy. Allow dish to sit for 10 minutes before serving.

NOTE: Additional grated ham and cheese may be sprinkled over the top before baking, if desired.

SERVES: 10

Athena Egg Salad In Pita Pockets

½ cup plain yogurt

½ tsp. salt

¼ tsp. oregano

6 hard cooked eggs, chopped

18 cherry tomatoes, quartered

½ cup (2 oz.) Feta cheese, crumbled

1 (2¼ oz.) can ripe olives, drained and sliced

¼ cup green onions including tops, chopped

4 pita pockets, halved

Anchovy fillets, optional

Blend yogurt, salt, and oregano. Stir in remaining ingredients except pita bread and anchovy fillets. Cover; refrigerate to blend flavors.

Fill each pocket with ½ cup egg salad. Garnish with anchovy if desired.

NOTE: May be served in a lettuce cup instead of pita pocket.

SERVES: 4

Blender Soufflé

Basic Ingredients:
1 Tbsp. butter, softened
6 eggs
½ cup heavy cream

For the Cheddar Cheese Soufflé:
¼ cup Parmesan, grated
½ tsp. prepared mustard
½ tsp. salt
¼ tsp. pepper
½ lb. sharp Cheddar cheese, cubed
11 oz. cream cheese, cubed

For the Roquefort:
1 tsp. Worcestershire
Dash Tabasco
¼ tsp. pepper
¼ lb. Roquefort or other blue cheese
11 oz. cream cheese, cubed

For the Ham:
1 tsp. Worcestershire
Dash Tabasco
4 tsp. tomato paste
1 tsp. prepared mustard
¼ tsp. pepper
½ lb. smoked ham, diced
11 oz. cream cheese, cubed

 Procedure for each soufflé is the same.

Butter a 5-cup soufflé dish or 5–6 individual baking dishes.

Place the basic ingredients, and all but last 2 ingredients for the version of your choice, in blender or food processor. Process until smooth.

Add the last 2 ingredients, piece by piece, while processing. When all ingredients have been added, whirl for a few seconds. Pour mixture into prepared dishes.

This souffle may be prepared, covered, and refrigerated for 1–2 hours.

Bake at 375° for 45–50 minutes for large dish or 15–20 minutes for individual dishes. Serve immediately.

NOTE: This soufflé may be served as an appetizer or as a main dish.

SERVES: 6

Ramekin Eggs

1. Eggs with Salsa:
1 tsp. butter, softened
1 slice Canadian bacon
1 Tbsp. salsa
1 egg
2 Tbsp. Cheddar cheese, grated

2. Cheese Baked Eggs:
1 tsp. butter, melted
1 tsp. cream
1 egg
Salt and pepper to taste
Havarti cheese, grated

3. Eggs Florentine:
1 tsp. butter, softened
1 Tbsp. spinach, chopped and steamed
2 tsp. Parmesan cheese, grated and divided
1 egg
1 Tbsp. heavy cream

EGGS #1

Butter 1 ramekin per serving. Stack the ingredients in each ramekin in the order listed. Bake at 350° for 15 minutes.

SERVES: 1

EGGS #2

Butter 1 ramekin per serving; add the cream. Gently crack a large egg into the ramekin. Season with salt and pepper. Sprinkle Havarti cheese on top.

Bake at 425° for 8–10 minutes, or until the white is firm and the center is still soft.

SERVES: 1

EGGS #3

Butter 1 ramekin per serving. Put chopped spinach in bottom, topped with 1 teaspoon cheese. Gently crack a large egg into the ramekin. Cover with heavy cream. Sprinkle with remaining cheese.

Bake at 350° for 8–10 minutes.

SERVES: 1

1895, Age 10

Mrs. Truman's Bing Cherry Mould (Salad)

1 large can bing cherries
2 packages cream cheese
1 package cherry Jello (or any red gelatin)
1 package lime Jello

Measure the juice from the cherries and add water to make two cups. Heat and dissolve cherry Jello in this. When partly set, add cherries.

Make lime Jello with water. When partly set, beat in cheese. Put cheese Jello in bottom of mould; let set; then put cherry mixture on top. Serve with mayonnaise.

ABOVE: Bess Truman was an avid sports enthusiast. Bess is shown here with friends in 1914 or 1915 at the Southern family tennis court on Park Avenue in Independence.

BELOW: Bess, far right, poses on horseback with her friends, Laura and Agnes Salisbury, in the early 1900s.

Champagne Fruit Salad

For the Sauce:

1¼ cups fresh or frozen raspberries

2½ Tbsp. sugar

1 Tbsp. fresh lemon juice

For the Salad:

4 small canteloupes

½ lb. strawberries, washed and hulled

½ lb. raspberries, washed

½ lb. blueberries or blackberries, washed

½ cup sugar

2 tsp. lemon juice

½ cup raspberry sauce

2 cups champagne or sparkling wine

SAUCE

Place raspberries in a food processor or blender; process until smooth. Push raspberries through a sieve into a bowl; discard seeds. Add sugar and lemon juice; stir until combined. Refrigerate.

YIELD: 1 cup

SALAD

Cut canteloupes in half and remove seeds. Using melon baller, scoop melon into balls and place in large bowl. Set aside melon rinds to be used as individual serving bowls; drain upside down on paper towels. Add berries to melon balls; toss gently. Do not stir. Sprinkle with sugar and add lemon juice. Chill 30 minutes.

To serve, fill each melon with fruit. Drizzle with 1 tablespoon raspberry sauce and ¼ cup champagne.

SERVES: 8

Pineapple Orange Salad

1 (20 oz.) can chunk pineapple or tidbits, drained

1 (11 oz.) can Mandarin oranges, drained

1½ cups seedless grapes

1 cup miniature marshmallows

1 cup flaked coconut

½ cup pecan pieces

¾ cup plain yogurt

 Combine all ingredients, stirring until well-blended. Refrigerate until ready to serve.

SERVES: 6

Papaya Kiwi Fruit Salad

1 papaya

4 kiwi fruit

6 Tbsp. frozen orange juice concentrate, thawed

3 Tbsp. honey

1 cup sour cream

1 Tbsp. orange peel, grated

1 Tbsp. lime peel, grated

 Peel and remove seeds from papaya. Slice lengthwise into thin slices.

Peel kiwi fruit and cut crosswise into thin slices. Arrange papaya and kiwi fruit on 4 salad plates.

Combine orange juice concentrate and honey in small bowl. Stir in sour cream. Spoon dressing over salads; sprinkle with peels.

SERVES: 4

Cheesy Fruit Salad

For the Dressing:

⅓ cup honey

1 cup yogurt

For the Salad:

2 cups pineapple, diced

3 apples, diced and sprinkled with lemon juice

3 oranges, peeled and sliced

2 bananas, sliced and sprinkled with lemon juice

1 cup seedless green or red grapes, halved

½ cup celery, chopped

½ cup dry-roasted peanuts

½ cup raisins

½ cup mild Cheddar cheese, shredded

 DRESSING

Blend honey and yogurt together; chill.

SALAD

In a large bowl, gently toss the salad ingredients; sprinkle with cheese. Chill.

To serve, gently combine dressing with salad.

SERVES: 4–6

Pineapple-Grapefruit Salad

1 (8½ oz.) can
  crushed pineapple,
  drained
  (reserve juice)
1 (12 oz.) can pink
  grapefruit, drained
  (reserve juice or
  use fresh)
1 (3 oz.) box
  lemon-flavored
  gelatin
1 cup celery, chopped
½ cup slivered
  almonds, toasted

Combine all reserved juice and enough water to equal 2 cups; bring to a boil. Add gelatin and chill until slightly thickened. Gently stir in remaining ingredients. Pour into ½-cup individual molds. Refrigerate until firm.

To unmold, place molds in hot water for 10 seconds. Gently turn upside down on a plate; remove mold.

NOTE: A 10–12 cup bundt pan can be used as a mold by doubling the recipe.

SERVES: 10

Filled Grapefruit Salad

2 grapefruit, cut
  into halves
2 envelopes
  unflavored gelatin
½ cup cold water
1 cup sugar
¾ cup boiling water
2 Tbsp. maraschino
  cherry juice
2 Tbsp. lemon juice
1 tsp. almond
  flavoring
1 (8 oz.) pkg.
  cream cheese
1 cup whipped cream
  Juice of 1 lemon
3 Tbsp. honey

 Keep grapefruit shells intact. Remove pulp and juice, reserving 3 cups.

Soak gelatin in cold water until softened. Add sugar and boiling water; cool until slightly thickened. Add 3 cups of grapefruit pulp and juice, cherry juice, lemon juice, and almond flavoring. Spoon into grapefruit shells. Chill overnight.

For dressing, combine cream cheese, whipped cream, lemon juice, and honey until smooth.

Prior to serving, cut each grapefruit shell in half and top with dressing.

SERVES: 8

Tropical Mini Fruit Salad

1 (30 oz.) can apricots, drained (reserve ½ cup syrup)

3 medium bananas, peeled

4 kiwi fruit, peeled, quartered, and sliced

6 oz. frozen orange juice concentrate

1 (16 oz.) can fruit cocktail, drained

 Place the apricots, syrup, bananas, half of the kiwi fruit, and frozen orange juice in a blender or food processor. Blend until smooth. Fold in the fruit cocktail and remaining kiwi fruit.

Place double paper liners in muffin tins and fill each with the fruit mixture. Freeze until firm. Remove salads from the tins. Allow 15 minutes thawing time before serving.

SERVES: 24

Frozen Fruit Salad

2 cups sugar

1 qt. buttermilk

⅛ tsp. salt

1 Tbsp. vanilla

1 (20 oz.) can crushed pineapple, drained

1 (17 oz.) can fruit cocktail or mixed fruit, drained

Mix first 4 ingredients well. Gently fold in fruit.

Pour into 9x13-inch pan and freeze. Cut in squares and serve.

NOTE: You may substitute 8 packets of artificial sweetener (Equal) for sugar.

SERVES: 12–15

Strawberry Grapefruit Salad

For the Dressing:

8 strawberries

1 cup oil

½ cup white vinegar

¼ cup pink grapefruit juice

⅓ cup honey

1 tsp. dry mustard

1 tsp. celery seed

1 tsp. paprika

For the Salad:

3 heads Bibb lettuce

3 pink grapefruit, peeled, quartered, and sliced

24 strawberries, halved

 DRESSING

Mix ingredients in blender and chill until ready to use.

SALAD

Break 1 head of lettuce into separate leaves. Arrange lettuce leaves on individual salad plates. Tear remaining 2 heads of lettuce into small pieces and divide torn lettuce onto salad plates. Place grapefruit slices on top of the lettuce. Top with 6 strawberry halves in the center of each salad.

To serve, drizzle with dressing.

SERVES: 6–8

Orange, Pecan and Onion Salad

For the Dressing:

- ½ cup olive oil
- ¼ cup rice wine vinegar
- 2 Tbsp. Balsamic vinegar
- 2 Tbsp. orange marmalade
- ¼ tsp. salt
- ¼ tsp. freshly ground black pepper

For the Salad:

- 3 heads Bibb lettuce, washed
- 4 fresh navel oranges, peeled and thinly sliced into rounds
- One small red onion, thinly sliced and separated into rings
- ¾ cup pecan halves, lightly toasted

 DRESSING

Combine olive oil, vinegars, marmalade, salt, and pepper in a jar; shake well.

SALAD

Arrange lettuce leaves on a large oval platter. Place orange slices and red onion rings in an attractive pattern on leaves; sprinkle pecan halves over all.

Do not toss the salad. Drizzle dressing over the salad and serve.

SERVES: 6

Winter Salad With Raspberry Vinaigrette

For the Dressing:

½ cup salad oil

¼ cup raspberry vinegar

1 Tbsp. honey

½ tsp. orange rind, grated

¼ tsp. salt

⅛ tsp. pepper

For the Salad:

1 head Bibb lettuce, torn into bite-size pieces

½ lb. fresh spinach, torn into bite-size pieces

2 oranges, peeled and sectioned

2 Red Delicious apples, unpeeled and thinly sliced

1 kiwi fruit, peeled and thinly sliced

½ cup walnuts, chopped and toasted

 DRESSING

Combine all ingredients in jar; cover tightly and shake vigorously. Chill.

SALAD

Combine all of the salad ingredients in serving bowl; toss gently. When ready to serve, toss with raspberry vinaigrette.

SERVES: 8

Strawberry Salad

For the Dressing:

- 1 cup mayonnaise
- 1 cup red wine vinegar
- ⅔ cup sugar
- ½ cup whole milk
- 2 Tbsp. poppy seeds

For the Salad:

- 1 head Romaine lettuce
- 1 bunch spinach
- 1 pt. strawberries, sliced
- 1 small Spanish onion, sliced into rings

 DRESSING

Blend dressing ingredients until smooth.

NOTE: Dressing can be stored in refrigerator for several weeks.

SALAD

Combine clean lettuce, spinach, strawberries, and onion.

Pour desired amount of dressing over salad mixture; toss and serve.

SERVES: 6–8

Feta Cheese Salad

For the Dressing:

1 Tbsp. Dijon
mustard

¼ cup red wine
vinegar

Salt and freshly
ground pepper
to taste

¾ cup extra virgin
olive oil

Parsley or
watercress for
garnish

For the Salad:

2 heads Bibb lettuce,
washed, patted dry

2 heads Belgian
endive, shredded

1 head radicchio,
shredded

2 carrots, cut into
matchstick pieces

1 yellow pepper, cut
into matchstick
pieces

1 red pepper, cut into
matchstick pieces

3 beets, cooked,
peeled, and cut into
matchstick pieces

1 cucumber, peeled,
seeded, and
coarsely chopped

1 tomato, cut into
½-inch chunks

4 radishes, sliced
paper-thin

¼ lb. Feta cheese,
crumbled

DRESSING

Whisk mustard, vinegar, salt, and pepper. Add olive oil.

SALAD

Scatter lettuce, endive, and radicchio on platter or individual serving plates. Arrange vegetables in rows on top of greens. Top with Feta cheese.

Drizzle dressing over salad; add garnish. Sprinkle with pepper as desired.

SERVES: 6

Raspberry Spinach Salad

For the Dressing:

½ cup raspberries

1 (8 oz.) pkg. light cream cheese

¼ cup raspberry vinegar or white wine vinegar

3 Tbsp. sugar

1 Tbsp. olive oil

For the Salad:

2 qts. spinach, torn

½ cup walnuts, toasted and chopped

1½ cups raspberries

 DRESSING

Place all ingredients in food processor; blend well. Chill.

SALAD

Combine all ingredients in large bowl; keep chilled.

To serve, drizzle dressing over salad mixture and toss lightly.

SERVES: 6–8

Caribbean Spinach Salad

For the Dressing:

1 tsp. Dijon mustard

2 cloves garlic, crushed

3 Tbsp. white wine vinegar

⅓ cup extra virgin olive oil

Salt and freshly ground pepper to taste

For the Salad:

¾ lb. fresh spinach

6 slices bacon, cooked and crumbled

2 ripe mangoes, peeled, pitted, quartered, and thinly sliced

1 cup cashews, toasted

¼ red onion, thinly sliced

 DRESSING

Combine mustard and garlic in mixing bowl. Stir in vinegar. Gradually beat in oil; salt and pepper.

SALAD

Rinse spinach under cold water; dry thoroughly. Pull leaves from stems and discard stems. Place leaves in salad bowl; add bacon, mangoes, cashews, and onion.

Toss with dressing and serve immediately.

SERVES: 4–6

BLT Salad

For the Croutons:
- 4 slices thick white bread, torn into ½-inch pieces
- 1 tsp. salt
- 1 tsp. freshly ground pepper
- 2 Tbsp. vegetable oil

For the Dressing:
- ½ cup mayonnaise
- 2 Tbsp. red wine vinegar
- 2 Tbsp. bacon drippings
- ¼ cup basil leaves, finely chopped

For the Salad:
- 1 head Romaine lettuce, torn into bite-size pieces
- ½ lb. lean bacon, cooked crisp, drained, and crumbled
- 1 pt. cherry tomatoes, quartered

 CROUTONS

In a large skillet, toss bread pieces with salt, pepper, and oil. Cook coated bread pieces over moderately low heat until golden brown.

DRESSING

In a small bowl, whisk together mayonnaise, vinegar, bacon drippings, and basil. Let stand, covered, at room temperature.

SALAD

In a large bowl, combine Romaine lettuce, bacon, and tomatoes.

When ready to serve, add croutons; pour dressing over salad and toss well.

SERVES: 4

Spinach With Hot Bacon Dressing

6 slices bacon
½ lb. spinach
2 tsp. sugar
½ tsp. salt
¼ tsp. black pepper
¼ cup cider vinegar
¼ cup water
2 Tbsp. onion,
   finely minced
1 cup canned
   pineapple chunks,
   drained

 Dice bacon and fry until crisp. Remove bacon from drippings and set both aside.

Rinse spinach under cold water and dry thoroughly. Pull leaves from stems and discard stems. Place spinach in a large bowl; sprinkle with the sugar, salt, and pepper.

Add the vinegar, water, and onion to the hot drippings. Heat until bubbly hot; pour over spinach and toss. Add the crisp bacon and pineapple; toss again. Serve immediately.

NOTE: May substitute ½ cup red bell pepper cut into strips or 1 cup sliced fresh mushrooms for pineapple.

SERVES: 6

Gourmet Salad

For the Dressing:

2 Tbsp. onion, chopped

3 Tbsp. cider vinegar

2 tsp. spicy brown mustard

½ tsp. sugar

½ tsp. salt

¼ tsp. pepper

1 cup vegetable oil

For the Salad:

½ lb. bacon, cooked and crumbled

1 bunch Romaine lettuce

1 (7½ oz.) can hearts of palm, drained and quartered

1 (8½ oz.) can artichoke hearts, drained and quartered

4 oz. Gorgonzola cheese, crumbled

DRESSING

Combine the onion, vinegar, mustard, sugar, salt, and pepper in a food processor. Process 5 seconds. Gradually add the oil in a thin, steady stream, processing continuously.

SALAD

Fry bacon, drain, and crumble. Tear the lettuce into bite-size pieces and place in large bowl. Add hearts of palm, artichoke hearts, and bacon. Toss with desired amount of dressing. Sprinkle with cheese.

SERVES: 8

Four-Leaf Salad

For the Dressing:

⅔ cup champagne
   vinegar

1 tsp. lemon rind,
   finely grated

2 Tbsp. fresh mint
   leaves, chopped

1 tsp. salt

   Freshly ground
   black pepper
   to taste

1⅓ cups extra virgin
   olive oil

For the Salad:

½ small head of red
   leaf lettuce

1 medium head of
   Boston lettuce

½ bunch of spinach,
   stems removed

½ small head of
   curly endive

   Lemon zest

 DRESSING

Combine the vinegar with the grated lemon rind, mint, salt, and pepper. Slowly whisk in the olive oil until well-blended.

SALAD

Wash and dry all lettuce, spinach, and curly endive. Tear into bite-size pieces and combine in a large salad bowl.

Just before serving, toss the salad with enough dressing to coat leaves. Garnish with lemon zest.

SERVES: 10

Mandarin Orange and Almond Salad

For the Dressing:
- ½ cup vegetable oil
- 2 Tbsp. malt vinegar
- 2 Tbsp. sugar
- ½ tsp. salt
- 1 tsp. Dijon mustard

For the Salad:
- 2 Tbsp. sugar
- ¼ cup almonds, sliced
- 3 cups head lettuce, torn into bite-size pieces
- 3 cups Romaine lettuce, torn into bite-size pieces
- 1 cup celery, chopped
- 5 green onions, sliced
- 1 (6¾ oz.) can Mandarin oranges, drained

DRESSING

Combine all ingredients in an airtight container. Shake until well-combined; chill.

SALAD

In a small skillet, melt sugar over low heat. Add almonds and stir constantly until completely coated. Transfer to a flat surface; cool and break apart. Set aside.

In a serving bowl, combine lettuce, celery, and green onions. Refrigerate.

Before serving, add Mandarin oranges to salad greens; toss with dressing. Add almonds and toss again. Serve immediately.

SERVES: 6

Romaine Salad

1 head Romaine
  lettuce
1 head Iceberg lettuce
1 large purple onion,
  thinly sliced and
  separated into
  rings, reserve some
  rings for garnish
1 (14 oz.) can
  artichoke hearts,
  drained
1 (2 oz.) can
  pimiento, drained
⅔ cup olive oil
⅓ cup wine vinegar
⅔ cup Parmesan
  cheese
¼ tsp. pepper
1 tsp. salt

Tear lettuce and combine other salad ingredients.

In a jar, mix oil, vinegar, Parmesan cheese, salt, and pepper for the dressing. Shake well until well-combined.

Pour over salad and toss. Garnish with reserved onion rings.

NOTE: Dressing will keep well in refrigerator.

SERVES: 8

Norwegian Red Cabbage

2 Tbsp. oil
5 cups red cabbage,
  shredded
⅔ cup sugar
⅓ cup white vinegar
1 tsp. salt
1 tsp. caraway seed

Heat oil in large skillet. Mix all of the ingredients and add to the skillet. Cover and cook on low until limp. Serve hot.

SERVES: 10–12

Freezer Coleslaw

2 cups sugar
½ cup water
1 cup vinegar
1 tsp. dry mustard
1 tsp. celery seed
1 Tbsp. salt
1 large head cabbage, shredded
½ cup celery, chopped
½ cup green pepper, chopped

 In a sauce pan, combine sugar, water, and vinegar; bring to a rolling boil. Cool; stir in mustard and celery seed.

Sprinkle 1 tablespoon salt on shredded cabbage and let stand for 2 hours. Wring out moisture; add chopped celery and green pepper.

Pour cooked mixture over cabbage. Divide into serving portions and place in ziplock freezer bags; freeze.

Allow to thaw 2–3 hours before serving.

NOTE: May freeze up to one month.

YIELD: 1 quart

Kelsey's Coleslaw Dressing

2½ cups Miracle Whip
½ cup white vinegar
1⅓ cups sugar
1 Tbsp. salt
1 tsp. celery seed
1 tsp. pepper
1 cup yellow onion, grated

Combine all ingredients; mix thoroughly. Store dressing in airtight jar.

Mix with cabbage ½ hour before serving.

YIELD: 4 cups

Salad Abilene

For the Dressing:
⅔ cup vinegar
½ cup oil
¾ cup sugar
1 tsp. salt
1 tsp. pepper

For the Salad:
1 bunch celery
1 bunch green onion
1 green bell pepper
2 (14.5 oz.) cans shoe peg corn, drained
1 (17 oz.) can early peas (Le Sueur), drained

 DRESSING

In a medium saucepan, combine dressing ingredients; heat until sugar is dissolved. Set aside.

SALAD

Chop celery, green onions, and green peppers into corn-size pieces; mix together. Add corn and peas.

Pour dressing over vegetable mixture and chill.

NOTE: This may be prepared 1 day before and will keep in the refrigerator for several days.

SERVES: 6–8

Red Potato Salad

For the Dressing:

8 slices bacon
2 tsp. Dijon mustard
1 Tbsp. sugar
2 Tbsp. vinegar
1 cup mayonnaise

For the Salad:

3 lbs. red potatoes
¾ cup celery, with leaves, chopped
½ cup green pepper, chopped
½ cup yellow onion, chopped

DRESSING

Dice and fry the bacon. Drain on paper towels and reserve.

Pour off drippings, reserving 2 tablespoons in skillet. Heat drippings slowly; add the mustard, sugar, and vinegar. Heat until the sugar is dissolved. Remove the dressing from the heat and mix in the mayonnaise until well-blended.

SALAD

Scrub the potatoes but do not peel. Cook in water until they can be easily pierced with a fork, but are not mushy. Drain the potatoes and slice into bite-size pieces while still warm. Toss with the vegetables and reserved bacon.

Pour the dressing over the warm potatoes and toss thoroughly.

SERVES: 10

Zucchini Salad

5 cups zucchini, chopped

½ cup green pepper, chopped

¼ cup onion, chopped

1 (4 oz.) can chopped black olives

1 (1 oz.) pkg. dry spaghetti or taco seasoning

½ cup salad oil

¼ cup vinegar

 Combine zucchini, green pepper, onion, and olives.

Blend spaghetti or taco seasoning with oil and vinegar. Pour over vegetable mixture and toss.

SERVES: 6–8

Insalata Allassio

12 slices tomato

12 slices Mozzarella cheese

¼ cup fresh basil, chopped

4 Tbsp. olive oil

1 Tbsp. wine vinegar

Salt and pepper to taste

 On a platter, arrange alternating slices of tomato and Mozzarella cheese.

Sprinkle with basil, drizzle oil and vinegar; salt and pepper.

NOTE: Great for a barbecue.

SERVES: 6

Oriental Broccoli Salad

4 cups broccoli, cut
  into small pieces

1 cup celery, diced

1 cup seedless green
  grapes, halved

1 cup seedless red
  grapes, halved

½ cup green onions,
  chopped

9 slices bacon, fried,
  drained, and
  crumbled

⅔ cup almonds,
  slivered, toasted
  if desired

1 cup mayonnaise

1 tsp. vinegar

⅓ cup sugar

 In a large bowl, mix together the first 7 ingredients.

Combine mayonnaise, vinegar, and sugar until smooth.

Toss with salad mixture and refrigerate until ready to serve.

SERVES: 4–6

Greek Salad

For the Mixture:
 1 cup parsley
 1 Tbsp. dried
 dillweed
 4 oz. Feta cheese,
 chilled

For the Dressing:
 1½ Tbsp. lemon juice
 ¼ cup extra virgin
 olive oil
 ½ tsp. dried oregano
 Freshly ground
 black pepper
 Salt to taste after
 salad is complete

For the Salad:
 2 small zucchini
 1 small cucumber
 3 plum tomatoes
 1 small red onion
 (about 3 oz.)
 1 cup large radishes
 Leaf lettuce
 Calamata olives

 MIXTURE

Put metal blade in workbowl of food processor. Mince the parsley with the dillweed by pulsing several times; leave in workbowl.

Break feta into 4 pieces; add to workbowl. Pulse to chop coarsely. Reserve the mixture; set aside.

DRESSING

Insert metal blade into empty workbowl. Pour in the dressing ingredients while machine runs. Leave in workbowl; remove metal blade.

SALAD

Insert 6x6 french fry disc. Stand zucchini in small feed tube. Process, using medium pressure on pusher. Leave each vegetable in workbowl until the finish. Continue with the 6x6 disc for the remaining vegetables: cucumber, medium pressure; tomatoes, position lengthwise and use light pressure; red onion, firm pressure; radishes, firm pressure.

Line serving bowl with lettuce. Invert workbowl into center. Add reserved cheese-herb mixture and toss gently to combine.

Garnish with several Calamata olives.

NOTE: Vegetables may be minced by hand, if desired.

• Calamata olives are usually found in your grocer's deli section.

SERVES: 8–10

Wild Rice Salad

6 oz. box Uncle Ben's
Long Grain &
Wild Rice

6 slices bacon, fried
and crumbled

3 Tbsp. bacon
drippings

1 Tbsp. flour

1½ tsp. salt

1 Tbsp. sugar

¾ cup water

½ cup vinegar

½ cup radishes, sliced

1 cup cucumbers,
sliced

1 small onion, sliced
and separated
into rings

1 cup celery, chopped

 Cook rice as directed and add bacon drippings.

Blend flour, salt, and sugar. Add water and vinegar. Cook over low heat until smooth.

Combine vegetables, bacon pieces, sauce, and rice. Toss until vegetables are coated.

NOTE: This dish is similar to German potato salad, but with rice.

SERVES: 6–8

Ramen Oriental Salad

For the Dressing:

½ cup olive oil

½ cup sugar

¾ cup cider vinegar

3 Tbsp. soy sauce

2 pkgs. seasoning
   mix from Ramen
   noodle pkg.

For the Salad:

2 pkgs. Ramen
   noodles, any flavor

10 cups cabbage,
   finely chopped

6 green onions, finely
   chopped

½ cup sesame seeds,
   toasted

½ cup slivered
   almonds, toasted

½ cup sunflower seed
   kernels, toasted

 DRESSING

Combine all ingredients in a glass jar and shake until well-combined. Refrigerate until ready to use.

SALAD

Crush Ramen noodles; set aside.

Wash and chop cabbage and onions; place in serving bowl and refrigerate.

In a shallow pan, toast sesame seeds, almonds, and sunflower seeds. Bake at 375° for 5-10 minutes or until lightly browned. Stir occasionally, being careful not to burn.

Before serving, mix all ingredients and toss with dressing.

NOTE: For a 1-dish luncheon, top with strips of Zesty Grilled Chicken (see page 221).

SERVES: 16

Salad Nicoise

1 lb. red potatoes, sliced ¼-inch thick

½ lb. whole green beans, ends snipped

⅓ cup lemon juice

2 Tbsp. cooking oil

1½ tsp. sugar

4 tsp. brown or Dijon mustard

¾ tsp. dried dillweed

2 Tbsp. water

¼ tsp. salt

⅛ tsp. pepper

Lettuce leaves

1 (6½ oz.) can tuna (water packed), drained and broken into chunks

2 medium tomatoes, seeded and cut into chunks

½ small red onion, thinly sliced and separated into rings

2 hard-cooked eggs, cut into wedges

In a large saucepan, bring 2 inches of water to boiling. Add potatoes and green beans. Cover and simmer 10 minutes or just until tender; drain. Cover and chill for 2–24 hours.

In a screw-top jar, combine lemon juice, oil, sugar, mustard, dillweed, water, salt, and pepper. Cover and shake well to blend. Chill for 2–24 hours.

To serve, place lettuce leaves on a platter. Arrange potatoes, beans, tuna, tomatoes, onion, and eggs atop lettuce. Shake dressing and drizzle over salad.

NOTE: If desired, substitute one 9-ounce package frozen cut green beans, thawed, for the fresh beans. Add to the potatoes during the last 5 minutes of cooking.

SERVES: 4

Luncheon Chicken Salad

For the Dressing:

½ cup sugar

¼ cup red wine vinegar

½ cup oil

1 tsp. salt

1 tsp. pepper

For the Salad:

1 head lettuce

5 green onions, sliced

1 (3 oz.) can chow mein or rice noodles

1 cup almonds, slivered

¼ cup sesame seeds

2 whole chicken breasts, cooked and cubed

 DRESSING

Combine sugar, wine vinegar, oil, salt, and pepper. Place over medium heat until sugar is dissolved; cool.

SALAD

Tear lettuce and combine with sliced green onions and noodles.

Toast almonds and sesame seeds in oven; set aside to cool.

Combine the above ingredients with the chunked chicken and toss.

Pour desired amount of dressing over lettuce mixture and serve.

SERVES: 4–6

Vegetable Chicken Salad

For the Dressing:

1 (10 oz.) jar Durkee's Famous Sauce

2 cups sour cream

5 Tbsp. mayonnaise

Juice of ½ lemon

1 tsp. dillweed

1 tsp. Worcestershire sauce

2 Tbsp. grated onion

Dash of Tabasco

For the Vegetables:

2 cups chicken broth

6 red potatoes, sliced thin

3 carrots, sliced

1 (14½ oz.) can green beans, drained

DRESSING

Combine all dressing ingredients and mix well; set aside.

VEGETABLES

In chicken broth, cook sliced potatoes and carrots until tender. Add green beans toward the end of cooking time; drain well. Drizzle with 2–3 tablespoons of dressing; cool.

For the Salad:

3 ribs celery, sliced

1 (10 oz.) pkg.
  frozen peas,
  thawed and
  well-drained

8 large mushrooms,
  sliced

6 radishes, sliced

½ green pepper,
  chopped

1 (8 oz.) can water
  chestnuts, sliced

1 (14 oz.) can
  artichoke hearts,
  optional

1 bunch green
  onions, sliced

5 cups chicken,
  cooked and cut into
  small pieces

1 (4 oz.) can black
  olives, sliced for
  garnish

SALAD

Place cooked vegetables in a large casserole. Top with layers of celery, peas, mushrooms, radishes, green pepper, water chestnuts, artichoke hearts, and green onions. Top with pieces of chicken. Pour dressing over all and garnish with olives.

NOTE: May be made the day before.

SERVES: 10–12

Basic Brown Sauce

4 Tbsp. butter

1 small onion, finely chopped

1 stalk celery, chopped

1 carrot, chopped

3 Tbsp. flour

2 Tbsp. tomato puree

1 tomato, finely chopped

3 cups beef stock

¼ cup dry sherry

1 bay leaf

Fresh parsley sprigs

Salt and pepper to taste

In a saucepan, melt butter; add onion, celery, and carrot. Cook until soft and lightly browned, about 5 minutes. Stir in the flour and cool for 2 minutes. Add tomato puree, chopped tomato, beef stock, sherry, bay leaf, and parsley. Simmer, uncovered, for 1½ hours.

Strain sauce; salt and pepper. The sauce may be used at once or cooled to room temperature.

NOTE: Brown sauce may be frozen for several months.

YIELD: 3–4 cups

Mushroom Wine Sauce

1 cup mushrooms, sliced
2 Tbsp. butter
½ cup Madeira wine
2 cups Brown Sauce (see page 122)
1 Tbsp. arrowroot
¼ cup cold water
   Salt and pepper to taste
2 Tbsp. unsalted butter

 Make this sauce with your favorite beef or pork roast.

Sauté mushrooms in butter and set aside.

Pour off fat from the roasting pan. Add Madeira and bring to boil, scraping all the brown bits on the bottom of pan. Stir in Brown Sauce and return to a boil. Strain into a saucepan. Dilute arrowroot with cold water and slowly add to sauce to slightly thicken; simmer for 10 minutes. Salt and pepper; whip in unsalted butter, a little at a time. Add sautéed mushrooms.

YIELD: 3 cups

Sauce Bordelaise

1 cup red wine
½ cup shallots, chopped
⅛ tsp. dried thyme
1 cup Brown Sauce (see page 122)
2 Tbsp. parsley, chopped
   Salt and pepper to taste

In a saucepan, combine the wine, shallots, and thyme. Bring to a boil over high heat. Cook briskly until the mixture has reduced to ½ cup. Add the Brown Sauce and simmer over low heat for 20 minutes; salt and pepper. Sprinkle with parsley.

YIELD: 2½ cups

Savory Sauce

1 onion, chopped

2 cloves garlic, minced

⅓ cup vinegar

2 Tbsp. Worcestershire sauce

1½ tsp. salt

1½ tsp. chili powder

½ tsp. pepper

1 can tomato sauce

½ can water

1 (10 oz.) pkg. frozen peas

Mix together all ingredients, except peas. Place meat, such as poultry or beef, in covered baking pan. Add desired vegetables (potatoes, carrots, celery, etc.) to pan. Pour sauce mixture over meat and vegetables

Cover and bake at 375° for 1 hour. Add frozen peas the last 15 minutes.

NOTE: This sauce may prepared in a saucepan and cooked over burner at low heat for 30 minutes. Serve over pasta, rice, noodles, or vegetables.

SERVES: 4

Minted Sauce for Meat

1 bottle chili sauce
1 (6 oz.) jar
  currant jelly
Few drops vinegar
Bud of garlic
Peppermint
flavoring to taste

 Combine all ingredients and cook 20 minutes, stirring occasionally.

Serve warm or at room temperature. Refrigerate.

NOTE: Especially good with roasted lamb.

YIELD: 1 cup

Jezebel Sauce

1 (10 oz.) jar apricot
  preserves
1 (10 oz.) jar apple
  jelly
1 (5 oz.) jar
  horseradish,
  drained
1 oz. dry mustard
1 tsp. ground black
  pepper

 Combine all ingredients well.

NOTE: Use to enhance meats of all kinds.

YIELD: Approximately 2½ cups

Mustard

1 cup dry mustard
1 cup malt vinegar
1 cup sugar
2 eggs, beaten well

Mix dry mustard and malt vinegar together until smooth. Let set several hours or overnight.

Mix with remaining ingredients and cook in double boiler until thick. Refrigerate.

NOTE: Will keep indefinitely.

YIELD: 2 cups

Tomato-Basil Mustard

4 Tbsp. dry mustard
¼ cup vinegar
⅓ cup white wine
1 Tbsp. sugar
½ tsp. salt
3 egg yolks
¼ cup tomato paste
½ cup fresh basil,
   chopped

In a saucepan, blend mustard with vinegar and wine. Add next 5 ingredients; cook until thickened. Do not boil.

YIELD: 2 cups

Dilly Sauce

½ cup Dijon mustard
2 egg yolks
⅛ tsp. salt
⅛ tsp. pepper
3 Tbsp. sugar
3 Tbsp. fresh dill, chopped
2 Tbsp. vinegar
6 Tbsp. olive oil

Beat first 6 ingredients until bubbles form. Gradually add vinegar, then drizzle in oil and beat until mixture thickens. Chill at least 4 hours.

NOTE: Keeps for several weeks.

YIELD: 1 cup

Tomato Basil Jelly

2 cups tomato juice
1 cup basil, medium packed
1 small, hot red pepper, optional
3½ cups sugar
½ cup lemon juice, scant
⅛ tsp. salt
½ pkg. Liquid Certo

Place tomato juice and basil in a large pan; add red pepper and bring to boil. Let simmer for about 30 minutes; remove from heat and let stand several hours. Strain and measure juice. Juice should measure 2 cups.

Return juice to pan; add sugar, lemon juice, and salt. Bring mixture to a full rolling boil (one that you cannot stir down). Add Certo and return to a full hard boil (one that you cannot stir down). Boil for 1 full minute. While still boiling, ladle into jars and seal with canning lids or paraffin.

NOTE: This is great served over cream cheese or on cornbread.

YIELD: 2 pints

Green Pepper Jelly Snacks

4 green bell peppers,
  hulled and sliced
4 green mild chiles
  (canned are okay)
1½ cups white vinegar
6½ cups sugar
1 bottle Certo
  Green food
  coloring
  Triscuits
1 (8 oz.) pkg.
  cream cheese

In a food processor, place green peppers, chiles, and vinegar (half at a time); process until smooth. Place mixture in a large pan; add sugar and bring to a boil, stirring constantly. Boil at least 12 minutes. Remove from heat and let cool 5 minutes. Add bottle of Certo and 5–7 drops green food coloring. Skim; pour into jelly glasses.

NOTE: If you use fresh green chiles, put in hot oven until they blister, then peel.

TO SERVE: Spread Triscuit biscuits with cream cheese and top with generous teaspoonful of Green Pepper Jelly.

SERVES: 4–6

Pickled Peaches

1 (28 oz.) can
  peach halves
1 cup sugar
¾ cup cider vinegar
1 Tbsp. whole cloves
1 Tbsp. whole
  allspice
2 cinnamon sticks

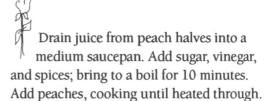 Drain juice from peach halves into a medium saucepan. Add sugar, vinegar, and spices; bring to a boil for 10 minutes. Add peaches, cooking until heated through.

Place peaches in bowl. Strain juice over peaches and refrigerate. Serve chilled.

SERVES: 4

Cranberry Relish

2 (3 oz.) pkgs.
  cherry-flavored
  gelatin
1 cup boiling water
2 lbs. cranberries
3 cups sugar
4 cups apples
1 (6 oz.) can orange
  juice concentrate
1 orange with
  some rind
1 lemon and ½ rind
2 cups nuts, chopped
3 cups celery,
  chopped

 Dissolve gelatin in boiling water.

In a blender, blend gelatin and all other ingredients, except celery and nuts. Fold celery and nuts into mixture. Refrigerate until serving.

NOTE: Recipe can be cut in half.

SERVES: 30

Celery Seed Dressing

½ cup sugar
1 tsp. mustard
1 tsp. celery seed
1 tsp. paprika
½ tsp. salt
1 cup salad oil
1 tsp. onion juice
¼ cup vinegar

Mix dry ingredients. Add oil (a little at a time), onion juice, and vinegar (1 teaspoon at a time). Beat for approximately 20 minutes or until mixture is thick.

NOTE: Dressing keeps well in the refrigerator.

YIELD: 2 cups

Sweet and Sour Italian Salad Dressing

1½ cups wine vinegar
1 cup sugar
2 pkgs. Good
   Seasons Italian
   salad dressing, dry
¼ cup oil
2 ice cubes

Bring vinegar to a boil. Remove from heat and add sugar, salad dressing mix, oil, and ice, stirring well. Chill.

Serve over mixed greens.

YIELD: 2 cups

1898, Age 13

Picadillo A La Ramos from Mrs. Truman's Spanish Class

1 pound lean round steak
½ pound lean pork
½ pound veal
2 cups dry white wine
½ cup raw, shelled almonds
1 cup pitted olives
1 cup raisins
2 large tomatoes
2 hardboiled eggs
2 cloves garlic
1 large green pepper
1 medium-sized onion saffron
    Several threads of toasted saffron
    Several sprigs of parsley
    Pinch of cumin seed
2 bay leaves
    Salt to taste

Cut the three meats into small pieces and grind together to mix well. Chop the tomatoes, garlic, onion and pepper and brown in a frying pan with a little butter. Add the ground meat to the pan and continue frying for ten minutes, stirring constantly. Put the contents of the pan into a pot with the almonds, olives, bay leaves, cumin seed, wine, and sufficient saffron to color the dish. Simmer for one hour, adding water as is necessary to keep the dish juicy. Add the raisins fifteen minutes before the end of the hour. Serve over white rice. Decorate each serving with two slices of hardboiled egg and a sprig of parsley. Serves six.

ABOVE: Bess Wallace enjoys a winter skate in the early 1900s.

Curried Avocado Soup

2 cups onion, chopped

2 stalks celery, chopped

¼ cup butter

2 Tbsp. flour

1 Tbsp. curry powder

2 tart apples, peeled and chopped

3 cups chicken broth, divided

1 cup water

1 chicken bouillon cube

2 avocados, peeled and chunked

2 cups light cream

Salt to taste

1 (4 oz.) pkg. frozen, tiny shrimp, thawed

½ cup coconut, lightly toasted

Sauté onion and celery in butter until translucent. Add flour and curry powder, stirring constantly until thoroughly blended.

Stir in apples, 2 cups of broth, water, and bouillon cube. Cook over low heat until apples are soft; cool slightly.

Transfer mixture to a food processor or blender. Add avocados; process until smooth. Combine cream, salt, and remaining broth; stir thoroughly. Taste and adjust seasonings. Chill thoroughly, preferably overnight.

Divide shrimp among soup cups. Add soup and garnish with a sprinkling of coconut.

NOTE: Toast coconut at 350° for 7–12 minutes, stirring frequently.

SERVES: 6–8

Elegant Artichoke Soup

½ cup green
  onions, chopped

½ cup celery,
  finely chopped

6 Tbsp. butter

6 Tbsp. flour

6 cups chicken stock

¼ cup fresh
  lemon juice

1 bay leaf

¼ tsp. red pepper

1 tsp. thyme

3 (14 oz.) cans
  artichokes, rinsed
  and drained

Lemon, thinly
  sliced for garnish

Parsley, finely
  chopped for
  garnish

In a large saucepan, sauté onions and celery in butter, until soft; add flour. Cook one minute, stirring constantly. Add stock and lemon juice; stir until well-blended. Add bay leaf and seasonings.

Separate drained artichoke bottoms from leaves; reserve. Add bottoms to soup. Simmer covered for 20 minutes; cool. Purée in food processor. Return to pan; add artichoke leaves, stirring until heated.

Garnish with slice of lemon and parsley.

NOTE: May be prepared in advance and reheated over low heat.

SERVES: 8–10

Cambridge Carrot and Ginger Soup

1 lb. carrots, cut into
   ½-inch pieces
1 medium onion,
   cut into quarters
1 medium potato,
   cut into chunks
1 qt. chicken stock
2 Tbsp. ginger purée
4 Tbsp. pure maple
   syrup
¼ cup heavy cream
   Salt and pepper
   to taste
   Scallions, chopped
   for garnish

 Cook carrots, onion, and potatoes in chicken stock until tender.

Make ginger purée by placing ginger and 1 teaspoon water in food processor. To ginger purée, add vegetables, stock, and maple syrup. Purée until smooth.

Return to pan and add heavy cream; salt and pepper. Simmer ½ hour; do not let the mixture boil. Serve hot; garnish with scallions.

SERVES: 12

Chilled Cucumber Soup

4 small cucumbers,
  peeled and seeded
1 (14½ oz.) can
  chicken broth
1 (10¾ oz.) can
  cream of
  potato soup
1 (8 oz.) carton
  sour cream
2 tsp. tarragon
  vinegar
½ tsp. salt
  Paprika
  Fresh parsley,
  chopped for
  garnish

Cut cucumbers into chunks to make approximately 2 heaping cups. Pour chicken broth into blender; add cucumbers and blend until liquefied. Pour into large bowl.

In blender, combine cream of potato soup, sour cream, vinegar, and salt. Blend until liquefied.

Combine cucumber mixture and sour cream mixture; stir with wire whisk until well-blended. Pour through tightly meshed colander. Refrigerate until well-chilled. Sprinkle with paprika and parsley.

SERVES: 4–6

Curried Pea Soup

1 (10 oz.) pkg. frozen peas

½ cup onion, sliced

1 small carrot, sliced

1 stalk celery with leaves, sliced

1 medium potato, sliced

1 garlic clove, crushed

1 tsp. salt

1 tsp. curry powder

2 cups chicken stock, divided

1 cup heavy cream

Place vegetables, seasonings, and 1 cup stock in a saucepan; bring to a boil. Cover; reduce heat and simmer 20–30 minutes, until vegetables are tender. Cool slightly.

Transfer vegetables to a food processor; purée. While processing, pour in remaining stock and the cream; chill. Garnish each portion with whipped cream.

To serve hot, omit adding cream in processor. Process purée and stock only; heat. Remove from heat; stir in cream. Garnish with a teaspoon of sour cream.

NOTE: May be made 2 days in advance.

SERVES: 4–6

Pumpkin Soup

1 (8–10 lb.) pumpkin with stem, reserving seeds

½ cup onion, chopped

1 cup fresh or canned tomatoes, skinned and chopped

½ cup water

1½ lbs. processed cheese (Velveeta), cubed

4 cups half & half
Salt and pepper to taste

4 cups seasoned croutons, divided

Toasted Pumpkin Seed Snack:

Reserved pumpkin seeds

2 Tbsp. oil
Salt to taste

Cut top off pumpkin and save lid to use as cover when serving. Scrape all seeds and membrane from cavity. While preparing soup, bake pumpkin at 300° for 30 minutes or until warm inside.

In a large saucepan, combine onion, tomatoes, and water over medium heat. Cook until onion is transparent. Add cubed cheese; stir until melted. Add half & half; season to taste.

Place 2 cups croutons in heated pumpkin shell. Add soup mixture. Bake filled pumpkin, covered with pumpkin lid, at 300° for 45 minutes to 1 hour or until steaming.

NOTE: To serve, carefully transfer pumpkin to large platter. Garnish platter with fall leaves, grapes, and red apple slices. At the table, ladle soup into heated bowls. Top with remaining croutons. Serve with bread sticks or crackers.

SERVES: 10–12

TOASTED PUMPKIN SEED SNACK

Reserve seeds from pumpkin, removing pulp and strings to clean thoroughly. Spread seeds in a single layer on baking sheet. Air dry for 3 hours. (Hull seeds at this time, if desired.)

When dry, add 2 tablespoons oil; add salt. Stir to coat evenly. Bake at 350°, stirring occasionally, until golden brown. Remove from oven; cool. Add more salt, if necessary.

NOTE: Great bridge snack!

Italian Tomato Soup

1 lb. Italian sausage

4 fresh tomatoes, chopped

1 (4 oz.) can Italian tomato sauce

7 cups beef stock

1 cup onion, chopped

1 clove garlic, minced

1 cup carrots, sliced

1 tsp. basil

1 tsp. oregano

2 cups zucchini, sliced

1 cup fresh mushrooms, sliced

1 green pepper, diced

¼ cup fresh parsley, chopped

2 cups frozen tortellini or small ravioli

1½ cups dill pickles, sliced

 In a large skillet, brown and crumble Italian sausage.

In a large stock pot, combine tomatoes, sausage, tomato sauce, stock, onion, garlic, carrots, basil, and oregano; simmer 30 minutes.

Add remaining ingredients, except pickles, and simmer an additional hour.

Before serving, add dill pickles and heat.

SERVES: 10

French Onion Soup

9 medium onions, sliced

¾-cup butter

4 Tbsp. flour

1½ tsp. paprika

12 beef bouillon cubes

9 cups water

1 cup Mozzarella cheese, shredded

1 cup Parmesan cheese, shredded

 Sauté sliced onions in butter until lightly browned. Add flour and paprika; blend well. Slowly stir in water and bouillon cubes; simmer 5 minutes.

Ladle soup into oven-proof bowls. Sprinkle with Mozzarella and Parmesan cheese. Place under broiler until cheese is melted. Serve with toasted French bread.

SERVES: 8–10

Baked Potato Soup

2 leeks, chopped

1 cup yellow onion, chopped

2 Tbsp. peanut oil

4 medium potatoes, baked, peeled, and chopped

6 cups chicken stock

Salt and pepper to taste

6 Tbsp. sour cream

½ cup Cheddar cheese, grated

¼ cup bacon, cooked and chopped

6 green onions, sliced for garnish

 Sauté the leeks and onion in the oil until translucent.

Add potatoes and cover with chicken stock. Simmer 20 minutes; salt and pepper.

Ladle into bowls. Whisk in 1 tablespoon of sour cream per serving. Garnish each bowl with cheese, bacon, and green onions.

NOTE: For more flavor, do not bake potatoes in foil.

SERVES: 6

Stuffed Spud Soup

2 lbs. frozen
  hash browns

½ cup butter, melted

¾ cup green
  onions, chopped

2 (10 oz.) cans
  cream of
  chicken soup

1 qt. half & half
  or milk

Salt and pepper
  to taste

2 cups Cheddar
  cheese, shredded

Fresh parsley,
  chopped

 Thaw hash browns overnight in refrigerator.

In a stock pot, sauté onion in butter for 2 minutes. Add soups, half & half, and potatoes; salt and pepper. Heat gently.

Garnish with cheese and parsley.

SERVES: 8–10

Vegetable Chowder Soup

4 cups chicken stock

4 medium red
potatoes, diced

1 medium yellow
onion, thinly sliced

1 cup carrots,
thinly sliced

½ cup green
pepper, diced

½ cup butter

⅓ cup flour

3½ cups milk

1 lb. sharp Cheddar
cheese, shredded

1 (2 oz.) jar diced
pimientos, drained

⅛ tsp. cayenne
pepper, optional

Freshly chopped
parsley, for garnish

 In a large stock pot, add chicken stock and vegetables; simmer, covered, until tender.

Melt butter in a medium saucepan over low heat. Add flour, stirring constantly. Cook and stir for about 1 minute until well-blended.

Gradually add milk. Cook over medium heat, stirring constantly until thickened and bubbly. Add cheese, stirring until melted.

Combine cheese sauce, pimientos, and cayenne pepper to vegetable mixture. Cook over low heat until thoroughly heated.

NOTE: Do not boil. Garnish bowls with sprinkle of fresh parsley.

SERVES: 12

Broccoli Cheese Soup

2 Tbsp. oil

¾ cup onion, chopped

6 cups water

6 chicken
   bouillon cubes

1 (10 oz.) pkg. fine
   egg noodles

1 tsp. salt

2 (10 oz.) pkg.
   frozen broccoli,
   chopped and
   thawed

½ tsp. garlic powder

6 cups milk

2 lbs. processed
   cheese (Velveeta),
   cubed

   Salt and pepper
   to taste

In a stock pot, sauté onion in oil. Add water and bouillon cubes; bring to a boil. Add uncooked noodles and salt; cook for 3 minutes.

Add broccoli and garlic powder; cook 4 minutes over medium heat. Add milk and cheese; salt and pepper. Cook until cheese melts, stirring constantly.

SERVES: 12

Canadian Cheese Soup

10 Tbsp. unsalted
   butter

1 carrot, peeled and
   finely diced

1 stalk celery,
   finely diced

3 green onions,
   including tops,
   thinly sliced

½ cup flour

3½ cups chicken broth

1½ cups light ale
   or beer

1 cup Parmesan
   cheese, freshly
   grated

12 oz. sharp yellow
   Cheddar cheese,
   grated

5 oz. white Cheddar
   cheese, grated

1 tsp. ground
   white pepper

2 Tbsp. green pepper,
   diced for garnish

2 Tbsp. red bell
   pepper, diced for
   garnish

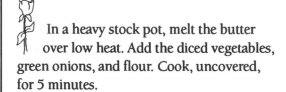

In a heavy stock pot, melt the butter over low heat. Add the diced vegetables, green onions, and flour. Cook, uncovered, for 5 minutes.

Add the broth and ale; bring to a slow simmer, stirring well.

Gradually whisk in the three cheeses and the white pepper. Simmer over low heat for 7 minutes. Do not boil.

Spoon into bowls; garnish with the green and red peppers.

SERVES: 6

Monterey Broccoli Soup

3 cups broccoli with
stalks, chopped

4 Tbsp. butter

¼ cup flour

1½ cups chicken broth

1 cup half & half

¾ cup Monterey Jack
cheese, shredded

Salt and pepper
to taste

Broccoli flowerets
for garnish

 Cook broccoli in salted water until tender; drain. Reserve flowerets for garnish.

Melt butter in saucepan and stir in flour until smooth. Gradually stir in broth, until thickened.

Add half & half, cheese, and broccoli; salt and pepper. Cook one minute. Remove from heat.

Garnish with broccoli flowerets.

SERVES: 4

Chile Con Queso Soup

1 cup butter
¾ cup flour
4 cups milk
2 (16 oz.) cans
  stewed tomatoes
1 (10 oz.) can
  tomatoes with
  chiles
1 medium green
  pepper, chopped
1 cup onion, chopped
1 cup celery, chopped
4 carrots, chopped
24 oz. processed
  cheese (Velveeta),
  cubed
  Light cream
  Sour cream
  Parsley, chopped

In a large saucepan, melt butter over medium-low heat. Stir in flour to make smooth paste. Add milk and cook over medium heat, stirring constantly until mixture boils and thickens. Remove from heat; set aside.

In a small saucepan, combine stewed tomatoes, tomatoes with chiles, green pepper, onion, celery, and carrots. Simmer over medium heat 15–25 minutes or until vegetables are tender. Purée vegetable mixture in blender or processor.

Combine puréed mixture with white sauce and place in slow cooker or top of double boiler. Add cheese; heat until cheese is melted and mixture is smooth. For proper consistency, stir in light cream to thin.

Spoon soup into bowls; garnish with dollop of sour cream and sprinkle of parsley.

SERVES: 12

Picadillo

½ cup white raisins

¼ cup beef broth

1 lb. ground beef

2 cloves garlic, crushed

½ cup onion, finely chopped

1 cup solid-pack canned tomatoes, drained and chopped

2 Tbsp. vinegar

1 Tbsp. brown sugar

1 tsp. cinnamon

¼ tsp. cumin

⅛ tsp. ground cloves

½ cup stuffed green olives, chopped

2 Tbsp. capers

Salt and pepper to taste

½ cup slivered almonds

 Heat beef broth in a stock pot; add raisins and soak until plump.

Sauté beef, garlic, and onion.

Add beef mixture and remaining ingredients, except almonds, to broth. Simmer at least 30 minutes until fairly dry. Sprinkle with almonds. Serve warm.

NOTE: Serve as a dip with tortillas or serve over rice for an entrée.

SERVES: 4–6

Hot Lime Chicken Soup

2 cups chicken broth

2 slices ginger root, ¼-inch thick

1 jalapeño pepper, cored, seeded, and minced

2 Tbsp. green onion, sliced, with tops

2 Tbsp. cilantro, minced, divided

1 tsp. nam pla (see note)

2 Tbsp. fresh lime juice, divided

1 chicken breast, boneless, skinless; cut into ½-inch pieces

Salt and freshly ground white pepper to taste

1 cup cooked rice

In a medium saucepan, combine chicken broth, ginger root, jalapeño pepper, green onion, 1 tablespoon cilantro, nam pla, and 1 tablespoon lime juice. Bring to boil over medium heat. Reduce heat to low and simmer 10 minutes.

Add chicken; simmer until cooked. Discard ginger slices and add remaining lime juice; salt and pepper.

Divide rice and ladle soup into each bowl. Sprinkle soup with remaining cilantro. Serve hot.

NOTE: Nam pla, also called fish sauce, is a Thai condiment available in Asian markets, and some supermarkets and specialty food stores. If it is not available, substitute 1 teaspoon soy sauce.

SERVES: 2

Tex-Mex Tortilla Soup

2 lbs. chicken
  breasts, skinned
  and boned

2 cups water

1 (14½ oz.) can
  beef broth

1 (14½ oz.) can
  chicken broth

1 (14½ oz.) can
  stewed tomatoes

½ cup onion, chopped

¼ cup green
  pepper, chopped

1 (8¾ oz.) can
  whole kernel
  corn, drained

1 tsp. chili powder

½ tsp. ground cumin

⅛ tsp. ground
  black pepper

3 cups tortilla chips,
  coarsely crushed

2 cups Monterey Jack
  cheese, shredded

1 avocado, peeled,
  seeded, and cut into
  chunks; optional

Snipped cilantro,
  optional

Lime wedges,
  optional

 Cut chicken into 1-inch cubes; set aside.

In a large saucepan, combine water, beef broth, chicken broth, tomatoes, onion, and green pepper. Bring to a boil. Add chicken; reduce heat. Cover and simmer for 10 minutes.

Add corn, chili powder, cumin, and black pepper. Simmer, covered, for 10 minutes.

To serve, place crushed tortilla chips into each bowl. Ladle soup over chips; sprinkle with cheese.

If desired, sprinkle top with avocado and cilantro. Serve with lime wedges.

SERVES: 6

Chicken Almond Soup

3 chicken breast
  halves
4 cups water
1 carrot, peeled
½ onion, quartered
1 celery stalk
6 Tbsp. butter
⅓ cup flour
1 cup milk
½ cup cream
⅓ cup sliced almonds,
  toasted
¼ cup dry sherry
  Salt and pepper
  to taste

Place chicken and water in saucepan. Add carrot, onion, and celery. Simmer 30 minutes or until chicken is tender.

Strain and reserve broth; discard vegetables. Chop chicken coarsely.

In a stock pot, melt butter over medium heat; blend in flour. When thoroughly mixed, add milk, cream, and 3 cups of the reserved chicken broth. Cook and stir until thickened.

Add chicken, almonds, and sherry; salt and pepper. Serve hot.

SERVES: 4 – 6

White Chili

2 lbs. chicken
    breasts, boneless,
    skinless

½ cup apricot brandy

1 lb. large white
    beans, soaked
    overnight in water,
    drained

6 cups chicken broth

4 cloves garlic,
    minced

2 medium onions,
    chopped, divided

1 Tbsp. oil

2 (4 oz.) cans
    chopped green
    chiles

2 tsp. ground cumin

1½ tsp. dried oregano

¼ tsp. ground cloves

¼ tsp. cayenne pepper

3 cups Monterey Jack
    cheese, grated

Place chicken breasts in baking dish with brandy. Cover and bake 30–40 minutes at 350° or until cooked. Cool and cut into bite-size pieces.

In a large stock pot, combine beans, chicken broth, garlic, and half the onions; bring to a boil. Reduce heat and simmer until beans are soft, 3 hours or more. Add more chicken broth, if necessary.

In a skillet, sauté remaining onions in oil, until tender. Add chiles and seasonings. Mix thoroughly; add to bean mixture. Add chicken; continue to simmer 1 hour. Serve topped with grated cheese.

SERVES: 8–10

Black Bean Soup

1 lb. (2¼ cups) dried black beans

2½ qts. water

1 lb. ham hock, cracked

2 stalks celery, chopped

2 cloves garlic, pressed

3 cups onion, chopped

½ tsp. pepper

¼ tsp. ground allspice

1 Tbsp. liquid beef broth concentrate (BV) or 3 beef bouillon cubes

1 (8 oz.) can tomato sauce

½ cup dry red wine

2 cups sour cream

1 lemon, thinly sliced

 Rinse beans, put in water and boil approximately 2 minutes, covered. Let stand for 1 hour.

Add ham hock, celery, garlic, onion, pepper, allspice, and beef broth concentrate. Bring to a boil; cover and simmer 2–3 hours. Remove ham hock and set aside.

Stir tomato sauce and wine into beans; blend in blender until smooth. Return beans to pot.

Remove ham from bone and place in soup; heat to a boil. Garnish soup with a scoop of sour cream and a lemon slice.

NOTE: The soup will be very thick.

SERVES: 6

Quick Bean Soup

1½ lbs. ground chuck

1 onion, chopped

3 (10 oz.) cans minestrone soup

2 (10 oz.) cans Rotel tomatoes and chiles

2 (15 oz.) cans Ranch-style beans

 In a stock pot, brown meat with onion; drain off fat.

Add soups, tomatoes, and beans. Simmer for 1 hour.

SERVES: 6–8

Tiffany Bean Soup

2 cups dried
   pinto beans
1 lb. ham, cubed
1 qt. water
1 (22 oz.) can
   tomato juice
4 cups chicken stock
3 cups onion,
   chopped
3 cloves garlic,
   minced
3 Tbsp. parsley,
   chopped
¼ cup green pepper,
   chopped
4 Tbsp. brown sugar
1 Tbsp. chili powder
1 tsp. MSG
1 tsp. salt
1 tsp. bay leaves,
   crushed
1 tsp. oregano
½ tsp. cumin
½ tsp. rosemary
½ tsp. celery seed
½ tsp. ground thyme
½ tsp. ground
   marjoram
½ tsp. sweet basil
¼ tsp. curry powder
1 cup sherry
   Green onions,
   sliced for garnish

 Wash beans and soak overnight; drain.

In an 8-quart stock pot, add beans, ham, and remaining ingredients, except the sherry. Bring to a boil and cook slowly until beans are tender, approximately 2–3 hours. Add sherry.

Serve in soup bowls, topped with chopped green onions.

NOTE: Preparing this soup ahead enhances the flavor. May freeze soup for up to six months.

SERVES: 8–10

Beef and Barley Soup

2 lbs. ground beef
or turkey

1 (16 oz.) can
chopped tomatoes

1 (6 oz.) can
tomato juice

7 cups water

½ lb. fresh green
beans, cut into
1-inch pieces

1 green pepper, diced

2 cups cabbage,
grated

2 cups broccoli
flowerets, diced

1 cup celery, diced

½ cup green
onions, chopped

Salt and pepper
to taste

2 tsp. garlic powder

2 Tbsp. light
soy sauce

1 bay leaf

½ tsp. paprika

½ tsp. thyme

½ cup pearl barley

3 carrots, diced

1 large potato, diced

In a stock pot, brown meat; drain well. Add the remaining ingredients, except the carrots and potatoes.

Bring to a boil and simmer for 45 minutes. Add carrots and potatoes; simmer for 30 minutes.

SERVES: 12–14

Lentil and Brown Rice Soup

5 cups chicken broth

3 cups water

1½ cups lentils, picked over and rinsed

1 cup brown rice

1 (32 oz.) can tomatoes, chopped and drained, reserving the juice

3 carrots, chopped

1 onion, chopped

1 stalk celery, chopped

3 garlic cloves, minced

½ tsp. dried basil

½ tsp. dried oregano

¼ tsp. dried thyme

1 bay leaf

½ cup fresh parsley, minced

2 Tbsp. cider vinegar, or to taste

Salt and pepper to taste

 In a heavy stock pot, combine all ingredients except last 3 items.

Cover and bring the mixture to a boil. Reduce heat and simmer for 45–55 minutes, stirring occasionally, or until lentils are tender.

Stir in the parsley, and vinegar; salt and pepper. Discard bay leaf. The soup will be thick and will thicken more as it stands. Thin the soup, if desired, with additional hot chicken broth or water.

SERVES: 8–10

Minnesota Wild Rice Soup

1 cup raw wild rice, soaked overnight

4 cups water

1 tsp. salt

2 tsp. curry powder, optional

2 cups onion, chopped

1 cup celery, chopped

½ cup margarine

¾ cup flour

8 cups water

9 chicken bouillon cubes

1 (4 oz.) can mushrooms, undrained

1 cup half & half

1 cup carrots, cooked and diced

⅓ cup fresh parsley, finely chopped

½ cup Cheddar cheese, grated for garnish

 Wash rice and soak overnight in cold tap water.

Place rice in a heavy saucepan with water and salt; bring to a boil. Simmer, covered, 45–55 minutes, until tender. Add curry powder, if desired. Uncover, and fluff with fork; simmer additional 5 minutes. Drain excess liquid.

While rice is cooking, sauté onion and celery in margarine until tender. Sprinkle with flour until the vegetables are well-coated. Mixture will be pasty. Slowly blend in water.

Add bouillon cubes, mushrooms, half & half, carrots, chopped parsley, and cooked rice. Simmer briefly to dissolve the bouillon cubes.

Ladle into individual bowls and sprinkle with grated Cheddar.

NOTE: May be made 1 day ahead. However, more liquid may be needed. Soup freezes well.

SERVES: 6–8

Chicken and Andouille Sausage Gumbo

1 tsp. salt
1 tsp. black pepper
1 tsp. white pepper
1½ tsp. cayenne pepper
6 chicken drumsticks or thighs
½ cup oil
½ cup flour
1 cup onion, chopped
1 cup green pepper, chopped
1 cup celery, chopped
7 cups chicken stock
1½ lbs. Andouille sausage, sliced ½-inch thick
1 tsp. thyme
1 pkg. frozen cut okra
½ cup parsley, chopped
½ cup green onions, sliced
4 shakes Tabasco
Filé powder, optional
Prepared rice

Mix salt and peppers together. Rub chicken with some of the mixture. Heat oil in a heavy stock pot. Brown the chicken lightly. Remove chicken and set aside.

Add flour to hot oil; cook, stirring constantly, until roux is dark red-brown. Add all vegetables and stir for 2 minutes; blend in chicken stock. Add chicken, sausage, remaining salt and pepper mixture, and thyme; simmer for 1 hour. Remove from heat.

Bone and skin chicken; cut into bite-size pieces and return to pot. Add frozen okra and simmer for an additional 7–10 minutes, until okra is cooked. Add the parsley, green onions, and Tabasco; heat briefly.

Serve in large soup bowls over rice.

NOTE: 1½ pounds of shrimp may be added or substituted for the sausage.

• Recipe can be made 1 to 2 days in advance.

• For extra spice, season individual servings with filé powder.

SERVES: 6–8

Heart-Healthy Gumbo

1½ lbs. turkey
  breakfast sausage
4 chicken breast
  halves, skinless,
  with bones
¼ cup olive oil
½ cup flour
2 cups onion, minced
1 large green
  pepper, minced
1 cup celery, minced
3 cloves garlic,
  minced
2 qts. water
3 tsp. Creole
  seasoning
¼ tsp. hot sauce
1 (16 oz.) can
  crushed tomatoes
1 tsp. dried basil
1 tsp. dried oregano
1½ tsp. salt
2 tsp. lemon juice
½ tsp. freshly ground
  black pepper
½ cup green
  onions, chopped
¼ cup fresh
  parsley, minced
  Hot cooked rice

Brown sausage in a sauté pan; drain and set aside. In the same pan, brown the chicken using medium-high heat. Remove chicken from pan and set aside.

Combine oil and flour in a stock pot. Cook over medium heat, stirring frequently, until roux is the color of chocolate, about 20–25 minutes. Add minced onion and next 3 ingredients; cook until vegetables are tender. Add water; bring to a boil. Reduce heat; simmer, uncovered, 45 minutes. Add chicken, Creole seasoning, and next 7 ingredients; cook uncovered, 1 hour.

Remove chicken and set aside to cool. Add green onions and parsley to gumbo. Bone chicken and coarsely chop. Add chicken and sausage to gumbo; heat thoroughly. Ladle gumbo into bowls; pack cooked rice into custard cups sprayed with non-stick spray; invert into bowls of gumbo, or serve gumbo over rice.

NOTE: Remove fat from surface of gumbo after it has been refrigerated 8 hours.

• Gumbo tastes better if fixed a day ahead. This gives flavors time to blend.

• Gumbo freezes well.

• Can add 1 lb. cooked, shelled, medium shrimp for additional interest.

YIELD: 3 quarts

Quick Crab Soup

3 (3 oz.) pkgs. cream cheese with chives

1 qt. half & half

1 (10¾ oz.) can cream of tomato soup

2 (10¾ oz.) cans cream of celery soup

1 lb. crab or imitation crab

½ cup dry sherry

1 cup sour cream
Fresh chives, chopped

In a 5-quart pan, combine cheese, half & half, and soups. Heat on low until warm, stirring occasionally with wire whisk. Add crab and sherry. Heat until steaming.

Ladle into bowls. Top with sour cream and sprinkle with chives.

SERVES: 10–12

Scrumptious Shrimp Soup

2 (10¾ oz.) cans cream of shrimp soup

2 (10¾ oz.) cans cream of mushroom soup

2 (10¾ oz.) cans cream of chicken soup

2 (10¾ oz.) cans Cheddar cheese soup

1 qt. half & half

1 (10–16 oz.) pkg. frozen salad shrimp

Combine all ingredients in a crockpot and cook on low-heat for several hours or until heated.

SERVES: 12

Oyster Bisque

¾ cup butter, divided

½ cup celery, thinly sliced

½ cup onion, julienned

⅔ cup flour

1½ qts. milk

2 pts. oysters, drained, reserving liquid

1 (7 oz.) can minced clams, drained, reserving liquid

Salt and pepper to taste

1 cup heavy cream, whipped

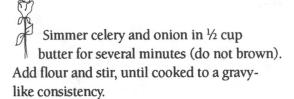 Simmer celery and onion in ½ cup butter for several minutes (do not brown). Add flour and stir, until cooked to a gravy-like consistency.

Heat milk slowly to warm.

Chop oysters; simmer in 4 tablespoons of butter for several minutes.

Add milk, oysters, minced clams, and reserved liquids to gravy mixture. Heat thoroughly, stirring gently; salt and pepper. Garnish each serving with scoops of whipped cream.

SERVES: 6

Maryland Clam Chowder

8 slices bacon, cut into 1-inch pieces

2 cups onion, diced

2 (7 oz.) cans minced clams, drained, reserving liquid

2 (8 oz.) bottles clam juice

4 medium potatoes, diced

½ cup celery leaves, chopped

3 Tbsp. butter

2 Tbsp. flour

1 qt. milk

2 tsp. parsley, chopped

Salt and pepper to taste

Sauté bacon and drain on paper towel. Pour off bacon drippings, reserving one tablespoon of fat to sauté onion.

In a medium-sized stock pan, sauté onion over moderate heat until transparent.

Heat the reserved clam liquid and the bottled clam juice. Add the potatoes, onion, and celery leaves. Cook until tender, 15–20 minutes.

Melt butter; add flour, stir until smooth, and slowly add the milk. Combine the white sauce and cooked vegetables with the clams, bacon, and parsley; salt and pepper.

SERVES: 8–10

Hungarian Goulash

¼ lb. bacon, cut into
  ½-in. pieces

3 lbs. beef (sirloin tip
  or top of round),
  cut into 1-inch
  cubes

1½ cups onion,
  finely chopped

2 cloves garlic,
  chopped

6 Tbsp. flour

4 cups water
  (may use some
  ginger ale)

2 (6 oz.) cans
  tomato paste

1 bay leaf

2 tsp. sugar

1½ tsp. salt

⅛ tsp. pepper

⅛ tsp. thyme

⅛ tsp. marjoram

2 tsp. paprika

 Fry bacon until crisp; remove from pan.

Brown beef, onion, and garlic in bacon drippings. Cook, stirring often, until onion is slightly browned. Sprinkle with flour and continue cooking until flour is brown. Add water, tomato paste, and bay leaf. Add sugar and remaining seasonings.

Cover and simmer 4 hours. Additional water may be added as needed.

NOTE: Serve over egg noodles or rice and garnish with parsley.

SERVES: 10

Vegetarian Stew

2 Tbsp. olive oil

2 large onions, halved lengthwise and thinly sliced

2 large cloves garlic, chopped

1 lb. turnips, peeled and cut into 1-inch pieces

1 lb. boiling potatoes, peeled and cut into 1-inch pieces

2 large carrots, halved and sliced ¼-inch thick

1 cup water

1 tsp. paprika

½ tsp. ground cumin

Dash cayenne pepper

Salt and freshly ground pepper to taste

¼ cup Italian parsley, chopped, divided

In a large, heavy sauté pan, heat oil over medium heat. Add onions; sauté about 5 minutes. Add garlic; sauté 15 seconds. Add turnips, potatoes, carrots, water, paprika, cumin, and cayenne; salt and pepper. Bring to boil, stirring. Reduce heat to low. Cover and cook, occasionally stirring gently, until all vegetables are tender, about 35 minutes.

Uncover and cook 2–3 minutes to evaporate excess liquid, stirring as little as possible. Lightly mix in 3 tablespoons parsley. Serve sprinkled with remaining 1 tablespoon parsley.

NOTE: The sweetness of sautéed onions and raisins is a good complement for turnips.

This recipe is also good when made with rutabagas. This is low calorie and high fiber— a heart-healthy dish!

SERVES: 2 as an entrée or 4–5 side-dish servings

Green Chile Stew

1 lb. pork, cubed
2 Tbsp. oil
½ cup onion, diced
   Garlic to taste
1 (16 oz.) can
   tomatoes, chopped
3 cups water
2 beef bouillon cubes
1 cup green chiles
2 medium potatoes,
   cubed

In a heavy stock pot, brown pork in oil with onion and garlic. Add tomatoes, water, bouillon cubes, green chiles, and potatoes. Simmer 1–1½ hours.

SERVES: 6–8

1901, Age 16

A Bess Recipe

Mrs. Truman's Meat Loaf

2 pounds ground beef
2 egg yolks
4 tablespoons parsley, minced fine
2 tablespoons butter
$^1/_4$ cup bread crumbs
3 tablespoons chili sauce
2 teaspoons salt
$^1/_2$ teaspoon pepper
1 teaspoon onion juice

For Basting:

$^1/_2$ cup melted butter
1 cup boiling water
  Parsley and radish roses (for garnish)
  Tomato sauce (can be bought in cans)
1 can frozen peas
  Butter

Combine the ingredients and shape in a loaf.
Butter a loaf pan, and place meat in pan. Bake in
a moderate oven (350°) for 1 hour, basting
frequently with butter and water combination.
Remove from loaf pan onto heated platter.
Garnish with sprigs of parsley and radish roses.
Serve with tomato sauce and green peas, to
which a dab of butter is added when served.

ABOVE: Bess and Harry, center, on a fishing trip during their courtship, circa 1913.

BELOW: Bess (far right) and Harry (seated in front) pose with friends at the waterworks near Sugar Creek, Missouri, 1913.

Veal Scallopini

5 Tbsp. butter, divided

4 Tbsp. oil, divided

1/4 lb. mushrooms, sliced

5 Tbsp. flour

1 lb. veal scallopini, thinly sliced

Salt and freshly ground pepper to taste

1/2 cup Marsala wine

1/3 cup heavy cream

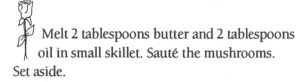 Melt 2 tablespoons butter and 2 tablespoons oil in small skillet. Sauté the mushrooms. Set aside.

Put remaining oil and butter in a large skillet and heat on high. Dredge the veal on both sides in flour.

Brown the scallopini quickly on both sides. Do not crowd. When the scallopini is done, transfer to a large platter. Season with salt and pepper.

Add wine to the pan and bring to a boil, stirring to deglaze pan. Add cream, stirring constantly until sauce thickens. Add sautéed mushrooms.

Over medium heat, add scallopini, one at a time, turning each one over in the sauce.

Transfer the scallopini and sauce to a heated serving platter.

SERVES: 4

Veal Parmesan

3 Tbsp. flour

½ tsp. salt

⅛ tsp. pepper

4 veal cutlets (¼- to ½-inch thick)

1 egg, beaten

2 Tbsp. water

⅓ cup fine bread crumbs

⅔ cup Parmesan cheese, grated and divided

½ tsp. dried leaf basil

3 Tbsp. oil

1 (15 oz.) can tomato sauce

1½ tsp. dried leaf oregano, divided

1 Tbsp. sugar

1 clove garlic, crushed

3 slices Mozzarella cheese

 In a plastic bag, combine flour, salt, and pepper; shake cutlets in mixture.

In a bowl, mix beaten egg with water. In another bowl, combine bread crumbs, ⅓ cup Parmesan cheese, and basil. Dip dredged meat into egg wash, then in crumb mixture.

Heat oil in a 9x13-inch dish; place cutlets in dish.

Bake at 350° for 30 minutes.

Mix tomato sauce, ½ teaspoon oregano, sugar, and garlic together; pour over meat. Sprinkle with the remaining ⅓ cup Parmesan cheese. Bake another 20 minutes.

Remove from oven and add Mozzarella cheese slices. Sprinkle with remaining 1 teaspoon oregano. Bake or broil 3–5 minutes more or until browned.

NOTE: Cube steaks may be substituted for veal cutlets.

SERVES: 4

Beef Tenderloin Florentine

1 (2½ lb.) beef tenderloin, trimmed

2 (10 oz.) pkgs. frozen chopped spinach, thawed

¼ tsp. salt

¼ tsp. pepper

⅛ tsp. allspice

½ tsp. dried thyme

1 clove garlic, crushed

½ tsp. sugar

2 cups boiling water

12 fresh pearl onions, peeled

12 button mushrooms, stems removed

1 Tbsp. olive oil

Using a sharp knife, make a small slit lengthwise down the length of the tenderloin. Continue cutting a little at a time, until meat lies flat. Be careful not to cut the meat in half. Pound the flattened meat with a meat tenderizer until it is about ½-inch thick; set aside.

Drain spinach and squeeze out excess liquid. Place spinach in mixing bowl. Add salt, pepper, allspice, thyme, and crushed garlic; stir well.

With the long side of the tenderloin toward you, spread the spinach mixture over the surface of the meat, leaving a 1-inch strip bare along the long side opposite you.

In a sauce pan, add sugar to boiling water; add onions and cook for 5 minutes; drain.

Alternately place the mushrooms and the onions near the edge of the long side of the meat closest to you. Gently roll up the meat so the vegetables are in the center. Secure the meat with cotton twine or with metal skewers. Brush with olive oil and place meat in baking pan.

Bake at 425° for 20–25 minutes, basting once or twice with the drippings until surface is brown and center is medium-rare. Roast an additional 30 minutes for well-done.

NOTE: Allow meat to cool 10 minutes before slicing thinly.

SERVES: 10

Beef Tenderloin With Horseradish Sauce

For the Beef:

1 (4 lb.) beef tenderloin
Soy sauce
Worcestershire sauce
Garlic powder
Salt and pepper to taste
4 slices bacon

For the Sauce:

¼ cup prepared horseradish, well-drained
2 tsp. prepared mustard
¼ tsp. salt
Cayenne pepper to taste
Paprika to taste
4 Tbsp. vinegar
½ cup whipping cream

 BEEF

Remove excess fat or skin from tenderloin.

Sprinkle meat with soy sauce, Worcestershire sauce, and small amount of garlic powder; salt and pepper. Fold the thin end under and secure with string.

Crisscross the meat with bacon slices. Let stand at room temperature for 3 hours.

Bake at 450° for 25–30 minutes, or until meat thermometer indicates desired doneness. Remove from oven and let cool at least 10 minutes.

SAUCE

In a small bowl, mix the horseradish, mustard, salt, cayenne pepper, paprika, and vinegar. Mix well.

In another bowl, whip cream until stiff. Gently fold whipped cream into the horseradish mixture.

NOTE: Make this sauce 1 day ahead to allow the flavors to blend.

SERVES: 12

Basil Tenderloin Filets

8 beef tenderloin
  filets, 1-inch thick
Salt and pepper
  to taste
2 Tbsp. butter
½ cup dry white wine
½ cup beef stock
1 cup whipping
  cream
⅓ cup fresh basil,
  chopped
1 cup tomatoes,
  peeled, seeded,
  and chopped
8 whole basil
  leaves, optional

 Pat meat dry and sprinkle both sides with salt and pepper.

In a heavy skillet, melt butter over medium heat. Add filets and cook to desired doneness, about 3 minutes per side for rare.

Remove meat and pour off fat; reserve, if desired. Add wine to skillet and bring to a boil to deglaze pan. Add beef stock; blend in cream and boil until thickened. Remove from heat. Add basil and tomatoes; blend well. For more flavor, reserved pan drippings can be blended in at this time.

Place beef on serving plate and pour sauce over beef. Garnish with basil leaves, if desired.

SERVES: 8

Red Pepper Tenderloin

2 (3½ oz.) beef
  filet steaks

1 tsp. oil

1 Tbsp. shallots,
  minced

2 Tbsp. fresh
  cilantro, finely
  chopped

½ medium red bell
  pepper, finely
  chopped

¼ cup Madeira wine

¼ cup beef stock

¼ cup plain yogurt
  Salt and pepper
  to taste

 In a non-stick skillet, sauté filets in oil to desired doneness. Remove and keep warm.

Add to skillet the shallots, cilantro, and red pepper. Sauté, stirring until pepper is just tender.

Add wine and increase heat to high. Reduce wine by half.

Add beef stock and bring to simmer. Whisk in yogurt and season to taste.

Pour sauce on serving plate and place meat in sauce.

NOTE: Delicious served with steamed vegetables and new potatoes.

SERVES: 2

Marinated Filet Mignon

6 filet mignon,
  2 inches thick

1 cup dry red wine

½ cup olive oil

2 Tbsp.
  Worcestershire
  sauce

¼ cup catsup

2 Tbsp. sugar

2 Tbsp. vinegar

1 tsp. dried
  marjoram

1 tsp. dried rosemary

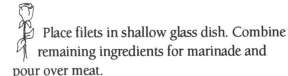 Place filets in shallow glass dish. Combine remaining ingredients for marinade and pour over meat.

Let stand at room temperature, 1–1½ hours, or refrigerate overnight.

Remove filets from marinade. Grill to desired doneness.

SERVES: 6

Elegant Steak

1½ lb. round steak, boneless and tenderized

1½ Tbsp. oil

2 large onions, cut in ½-inch slices

1 (10¾ oz.) can cream of mushroom soup

½ cup cooking sherry

1½ tsp. garlic salt

1 (4 oz.) can sliced mushrooms, drained; reserve liquid

 Partially freeze steak and cut into thin strips.

In a large skillet, heat oil; add meat and cook on high to brown meat; add onions which have been separated into rings. Sauté until onions are tender.

In a large bowl, blend soup, sherry, garlic salt, and reserved mushroom liquid.

Pour soup mixture over steak; add sliced mushrooms. Reduce heat; cover and simmer on low for 1 hour or until steak is tender.

Serve over rice, mashed potatoes, or pasta.

NOTE: This dish may also be prepared in oven. After browning steak, place in baking dish; add sauce and mushrooms and bake at 350° for 1 hour.

SERVES: 6

Teriyaki Kabob

½ cup chutney

2½ cups catsup

⅓ cup soy sauce

1 clove garlic, mashed

3 Tbsp. lemon juice

2 Tbsp. salad oil

3 lbs. sirloin tip, 1-inch cubes

12 fresh pineapple chunks

2 green peppers, cut into chunks

1 (16 oz.) can boiled onions

Combine chutney, catsup, soy sauce, garlic, lemon juice, and oil; blend until sauce is smooth.

Fill skewer by alternating sirloin tip, pineapple, green pepper, and boiled onions. Place filled skewers in a pan and brush with the sauce.

Chill skewers for 4 hours. Let stand at room temperature for 1 hour. Grill 8–10 minutes on each side, basting with remaining sauce.

SERVES: 6–8

Steak With Wild Rice

Ingredients

3 Tbsp. flour, divided

1½ tsp. salt, divided

⅛ tsp. pepper

1½ lbs. round steak,
1-inch thick

3 Tbsp. butter,
divided

¼ cup onion,
finely chopped

½ cup tomato juice

¾ cup wild rice,
cooked

¼ cup parsley,
finely chopped

2 Tbsp. shortening

½ cup water

1 cup fresh
mushrooms, diced

 In a small bowl, combine 2 tablespoons flour, 1 teaspoon salt, and pepper. Pound mixture into round steak on both sides; set aside.

In a skillet, melt 2 tablespoons butter and sauté onion until soft. Stir in remaining tablespoon flour and ½ teaspoon salt. Add tomato juice. Cook over low heat until thickened. Add cooked rice and parsley.

Spread stuffing mixture on steak. Roll and fasten with skewers. Brown rolled meat in shortening and transfer to an oven-proof dish.

Add water and bake, covered, at 350° for 2 hours.

In small skillet, sauté mushrooms in 1 tablespoon butter and garnish steak.

SERVES: 6

Speedy Stroganoff

1½ lbs. round steak
2 Tbsp. flour
1 tsp. paprika
½ tsp. salt
⅛ tsp. pepper
1 medium onion, sliced
1 (4 oz.) can sliced mushrooms, drained
2 Tbsp. butter
1 (10¾ oz.) can beef gravy
½ cup sour cream

 Cut steak into thin strips; dust with mixture of flour, paprika, salt, and pepper.

In skillet, brown meat, onion, and mushrooms in butter. Add beef gravy. Cover; cook over low heat for about 1½ hours. (If desired, cook uncovered the last 15 minutes to thicken gravy.) Stir occasionally.

Blend in sour cream just before serving.

NOTE: Serve with buttered noodles.

SERVES: 4–6

No-Peek Stew Bake

2 lbs. stew meat
1 pkg. dry onion soup mix
1 (10½ oz.) can cream of mushroom soup
1 (2½ oz.) can mushrooms, drained
1 cup ginger ale or water

 Place meat in baking dish. Mix other ingredients and pour over meat.

Cover and bake at 350° for 2–3 hours. Do not peek!

NOTE: Serve over noodles, rice, or mashed potatoes.

SERVES: 6–8

French Dip Sandwiches

1 (5 lb.) rump roast
2 pkgs. au jus mix
2 pkgs. Italian salad
  dressing mix
2 (10½ oz.) cans
  beef broth
1½ cans water
  Sourdough buns

Place roast in crockpot. Mix next 4 ingredients and pour over roast. Cook 8 hours on low. Remove roast and cool before slicing. Reserve juice for serving.

Slice meat as thinly as possible. Pile the meat on sourdough buns; wrap in foil and heat at 350° until warm. Serve on individual plates with a cup of au jus on the side for dipping.

NOTE: For a smaller roast, halve amounts. May be roasted in covered heavy pan in oven, but reduce cooking time to 4 hours at 325°.

SERVES: 12

Garbage Can Dinner

24 ears of corn,
   shucked, cut in half
1 (5 lb.) boneless
   beef roast, seasoned
   as desired
4 lbs. Polish sausage
3 lbs. Knockwurst
3 lbs. Bratwurst
2 lbs. hot dogs
10 lbs. red potatoes,
   scrubbed
3 lbs. carrots, peeled
2 bunches celery,
   cut in half
2 medium heads of
   cabbage, quartered
3 cans of beer
1 carrot to check
   for doneness

 Build wood fire and place grate on fire.

Place a new metal garbage can, 15-inch diameter at bottom, on the grate. (Can should be soldered to prevent leaking.) Pour 6 inches of water in the can. Hang a grill inside can above the water, using coat hanger.

Line grill with ears of corn. Layer meats and vegetables on top in the order given.

Pour beer over the top and add more beer as needed during cooking.

Cook approximately 3 hours. Taste carrot to test for doneness.

SERVES: 24

Twin Meat Loaves

1½ lbs. ground beef
½ lb. ground pork
¼ cup onion, finely
   chopped
2 Tbsp. celery, finely
   chopped
2 tsp. salt
½ tsp. poultry
   seasoning
¼ tsp. pepper
¼ tsp. dry mustard
1 Tbsp.
   Worcestershire
   sauce
4 slices soft bread,
   cubed
½ cup milk
2 eggs
½ cup dry bread
   crumbs
1 cup chili sauce
½ cup boiling water

 In a large bowl, thoroughly mix meats. Stir in the onion, celery, and seasonings.

In a small bowl, soak bread cubes in milk; add eggs. Beat with rotary mixer.

Combine meat and egg mixtures. Form into 2 loaves; roll in dry bread crumbs.

Place loaves in a greased shallow baking pan or jelly roll pan. Spread ½ cup chili sauce over each loaf. Pour boiling water around loaves.

Bake uncovered at 350° for 1 hour. Baste with liquid in pan at 15-minute intervals.

Serve hot or chilled.

SERVES: 8–10

Rolled Mozzarella Meat Loaf

1 (8 oz.) can tomato sauce

1 Tbsp. Parmesan cheese, grated

1 Tbsp. Romano cheese, grated

3 lbs. ground chuck

2 eggs

1 tsp. garlic powder

1½ tsp. Italian seasoning

½ cup onion, chopped

1 cup bread crumbs, dried

Salt and pepper to taste

8 oz. Mozzarella cheese, shredded

 Combine the tomato sauce, Parmesan cheese, and Romano cheese; set aside.

Mix ground chuck, eggs, garlic powder, Italian seasoning, onion, bread crumbs, and half of the tomato sauce mixture; salt and pepper.

Place meat mixture between two sheets of waxed paper and roll the meat out to a 9x12-inch rectangle. Remove top sheet of paper. Sprinkle the shredded Mozzarella over the meat leaving a ½-inch border all around. Working from a long side, roll up the meat like a jelly roll. Press seam to seal. Place seam side down in 9x13-inch pan.

Bake at 350° for 1 hour.

Pour remaining sauce over top and bake 15 minutes more.

NOTE: May be served with mushroom gravy.

SERVES: 12

Eldorado Meat Loaf

2½ lbs. ground beef
½ cup onion, chopped
1 (10¾ oz.) can
    cream of chicken
    soup
1 (10¾ oz.) can
    cream of
    tomato soup
1 (10¾ oz.) can
    cream of
    mushroom soup
1 can water
1½ cups instant rice,
    uncooked
1 pkg. taco seasoning
1 (8 oz.) jar
    taco sauce
1 (7 oz.) can diced
    tomatoes and
    green chiles
1 (10 oz.) bag cheese
    or corn flavored
    tortilla chips,
    crushed
2 cups Cheddar
    cheese, grated

 In a large skillet, brown ground beef and onion; drain.

Combine soups, water, rice, taco seasoning, taco sauce, and tomatoes in large saucepan. Cook over medium heat until bubbly; add ground beef.

In a 9x13-inch baking dish, alternate layers of chips, meat mixture, and cheese, making cheese the final layer.

Bake at 450° for 20 minutes.

SERVES: 6–8

Taco Pie

2 lbs. ground beef
1 pkg. taco seasoning
1 cup water
1 cup onion, chopped
1 (8 oz.) can
  crescent rolls
2 cups corn chips,
  crushed
1 (8 oz.) carton
  sour cream
1 cup Cheddar
  cheese, grated
Lettuce and
  tomato, chopped
Sliced olives,
  optional
Taco sauce

 In a large skillet, brown ground beef; add taco seasoning, water, and onion.

Separate crescent rolls and press in a 9-inch deep-dish pie pan. Pinch perforations together to make crust.

Layer in order: 1 cup corn chips, ground beef mixture, sour cream, and remaining corn chips. Top with grated cheese.

Bake at 350° for 20–25 minutes.

Serve with lettuce, tomatoes, olives, and taco sauce.

SERVES: 6–8

San Clemente Pie

1 lb. ground beef
½ cup onion, chopped
2 small boxes
   cornbread mix
1 cup cottage cheese
1 cup milk
1 egg, beaten
¼ lb. margarine
1 (15 oz.) can
   cream-style corn
   Diced jalapeño
   peppers, optional
½ cup Cheddar
   cheese, grated

 Brown ground beef and onion; drain and set aside.

Mix together remaining ingredients, except cheese.

Place half of cornbread mixture into greased 9x13-inch dish. Spoon ground beef and onion over cornbread mixture. Cover with remaining cornbread mixture.

Sprinkle cheese over top.

Bake at 350° for 1 hour.

SERVES: 8–10

Beef and Zucchini Casserole

1 lb. ground beef
2 lbs. zucchini, sliced
¼ cup onion, chopped
1 Tbsp. butter
1 (10½ oz.) can cream of chicken soup
1 cup dairy sour cream
1 cup carrots, grated
2 cups seasoned stuffing mix
¼ cup butter, melted
1 cup Cheddar cheese, grated

 Brown ground beef and drain fat.

Sauté zucchini and onion in 1 tablespoon of butter. Combine soup, sour cream, and carrots; add to zucchini and onion.

Toss stuffing mix with ¼ cup melted butter.

Layer beef, soup mixture, and stuffing mix in 9x13-inch dish, ending with stuffing mix.

Bake at 350° for 25 minutes.

Sprinkle with grated cheese and bake an additional 10 minutes or until cheese melts.

SERVES: 6–8

Ham Rollups

1 cup fresh
   bread crumbs
½ cup milk
1½ lbs. ground
   round beef
2 tsp. instant rice
1½ tsp. Worcestershire
   sauce
2 tsp. seasoned salt
¼ tsp. pepper
6 slices boiled ham
18 whole cloves
3 Tbsp. butter
⅔ cup brown sugar
½ cup orange juice
2 tsp. prepared
   mustard
1 (16 oz.) can
   apricot halves,
   drained
1 (8 oz.) can peach
   slices, drained
½ cup pineapple
   chunks, drained
1 (8 oz.) can green
   grapes, optional

In a large bowl, soak bread crumbs in milk; add ground beef, rice, and the next 3 seasonings. Mix well.

Divide beef mixture into 6 equal portions; pat into oblong shapes the size of the ham slices. Place the formed patties on the center of the ham slices; wrap ham tightly around the mixture and place seam side down in greased oblong baking dish.

Stud 3 whole cloves in each ham roll; set aside.

In a small saucepan, melt butter. Add sugar and orange juice; cook until sugar is dissolved. Stir in mustard.

Pour sauce over ham rolls and bake, uncovered, at 350° for 45 minutes.

While the rolls bake, combine the 4 canned fruits. At the end of the 45 minutes, remove dish from oven. Top rolls with fruit and bake, uncovered, 10 minutes longer.

SERVES: 6

Pork Tenderloin Waldorf

2 pork tenderloins
(1½ lbs.)

¾ cup apple jelly

¼ cup lemon juice
concentrate

¼ cup soy sauce

¼ cup oil

1 Tbsp. ginger root,
grated

1 cup apple, chopped

1 cup fresh
bread crumbs

¼ cup celery, chopped

¼ cup pecans,
chopped

Apple wedges

Parsley sprigs

Partially slit tenderloins lengthwise, being careful not to cut all the way through. Place tenderloins in zippered plastic bag; set aside.

In a small saucepan, combine jelly, lemon juice, soy sauce, oil, and ginger root. Cook and stir until jelly melts; reserve 3 tablespoons.

Carefully pour jelly mixture over tenderloins and seal bag. Refrigerate 4 hours or overnight.

When ready to cook, combine the apple, bread crumbs, celery, pecans, and reserved jelly mixture in a small bowl.

Place tenderloins in baking dish; spoon apple mixture into the slits of tenderloins.

Bake at 350° for 30 minutes. Loosely cover and bake 10 minutes longer or until meat thermometer reaches 160°. Garnish with apple wedges and parsley.

SERVES: 4–6

Pork Loin Braised in Milk

2 Tbsp. butter
2 Tbsp. oil
2 lbs. pork loin
1 tsp. salt
    Pepper to taste
2½ cups milk, divided
3 Tbsp. warm water

Heat the butter and oil over medium heat in a pan just large enough to contain the pork. Brown meat thoroughly on all sides, lowering heat if butter starts to turn dark brown.

Salt and pepper meat; slowly add 1 cup milk. After the milk comes to a boil, turn the heat down to medium-low. Cover loosely and cook slowly for about 2 hours, turning the meat several times. Add the remaining milk after the milk in pan has reached a nice brown color.

When meat is cooked, the milk should have coagulated into small nut-brown clusters. If it is still pale in color, uncover the pot, raise the heat to high, and cook briskly until it darkens. Better browning results will be achieved using a higher fat-content milk.

Remove the meat to a cutting board and let cool. Carve into slices ⅜-inch thick and place on warm platter.

Draw off most of the fat from the pan with a spoon and discard, being careful not to discard any of the coagulated milk clusters. Add 2–3 tablespoons warm water; turn heat to high and boil away the water while deglazing pan. Spoon sauce over sliced pork and serve immediately.

NOTE: Pork cooked by this method turns out to be exceptionally tender and juicy.

SERVES: 6–8

Pork Loin Roast

1 (8 oz.) jar
   Dijon mustard
1 cup olive oil
   Juice of 1 lemon
1 tsp. thyme
   Salt and pepper
   to taste
1 (5 lb.) pork loin
   roast, boned,
   rolled, and tied

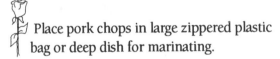 In a small bowl, combine mustard, olive oil, lemon juice, and thyme; salt and pepper. Pour over roast. Cover and refrigerate. Marinate for 24 hours, turning occasionally.

Remove meat, reserving marinade. Roast at 350° for 2½ hours or until meat thermometer inserted in center of roast reaches 160°.

Baste roast last 30 minutes with reserved meat marinade.

SERVES: 8–10

Party Pork Chops

6 pork chops,
   1-inch thick
¼ cup soy sauce
½ cup dry vermouth
2 Tbsp.
   Worcestershire
   sauce
2 Tbsp. Kitchen
   Bouquet
2 tsp. garlic salt
   Seasoned pepper
   to taste

Place pork chops in large zippered plastic bag or deep dish for marinating.

In a small bowl, combine the soy sauce, vermouth, Worcestershire sauce, Kitchen Bouquet, garlic salt, and seasoned pepper. Pour all but ¼ cup over pork chops and marinate 2–3 hours in refrigerator.

Place chops on heated grill and brown on each side for 3 minutes. Move from direct heat and continue grilling 30–35 minutes. Baste with remaining marinade while cooking.

SERVES: 6

Cötelettes de Porc

½ cup flour
1 tsp. salt
¼ tsp. pepper
½ tsp. thyme
6 pork chops, butterflied
2 Tbsp. butter
2 Tbsp. olive oil
1 cup dry vermouth
½ lb. mushrooms, sliced
6 slices Swiss or Muenster cheese
Parsley

In a shallow dish, combine flour, salt, pepper, and thyme. Dredge pork chops in flour mixture.

In a heavy skillet, heat butter and olive oil over medium heat. Cook pork chops until golden brown on both sides. Drain fat from skillet; add vermouth. Cover and simmer for 45–60 minutes or until tender. If necessary, add more vermouth diluted with water to keep chops from sticking.

Add mushrooms to skillet 20 minutes before serving.

Place cheese slices over chops 10 minutes before serving.

Garnish with parsley and serve.

NOTE: May use pork cutlets or boneless skinless chicken breasts.

SERVES: 6

Grilled Blue Cheese Stuffed Chops

For the Stuffing:

½ cup carrots, shredded

¼ cup pecans, chopped

¼ cup blue cheese, crumbled

1 green onion, thinly sliced

1 tsp. Worcestershire sauce

For the Chops:

4 pork loin rib chops, cut 1½-inch thick

1 recipe blue cheese stuffing

1 recipe creamy sauce

Crumbled blue cheese, optional

For the Sauce:

4 tsp. flour

¼ cup plain yogurt

¾ cup milk

½ tsp. instant chicken bouillon

⅛ tsp. pepper

 STUFFING

In a mixing bowl, combine the carrots, pecans, blue cheese, onion, and Worcestershire sauce.

CHOPS

Trim any fat from chops; cut a pocket in each chop from fat side almost to the bone. Spoon about ¼ cup of the blue cheese stuffing into each pocket; close pocket with wooden picks.

In a covered grill, arrange hot coals around drip pan over medium heat. Place chops over drip pan. Cover; grill about 40 minutes or until no pink remains.

Top chops with creamy sauce and sprinkle with blue cheese, if desired.

SAUCE

In a small saucepan, stir flour into yogurt over low heat. Add milk, chicken bouillon, and pepper. Cook until thickened and bubbly.

SERVES: 4

Barbito Burritos

2 lbs. pork, cubed

1 tsp. garlic, minced

Salt and pepper
to taste

4 Tbsp. flour

1 (16 oz.) can
stewed tomatoes

2 (4 oz.) cans diced
green chiles

3½ cups water

5 cups cooked
pinto beans
(or 2½ cups dry)

2 cups Cheddar
cheese, grated

Salsa to taste

12 (10-inch) flour
tortillas, warmed

To prepare green chile gravy, brown pork in skillet with garlic; salt and pepper. Add flour and brown lightly.

Add tomatoes, chiles, and water. Bring to boil; reduce heat and simmer 2 hours.

For bean mixture, mash cooked beans with potato masher; add grated cheese and heat until cheese is melted. Add ⅓ cup green chile gravy and salsa to taste.

Spread ½ cup of bean mixture on each tortilla; roll tortilla and place seam side down on platter. Cover burritos with remaining green chile gravy and serve.

SERVES: 12

Dilled Salmon With Spinach

2 (4 oz.) salmon
  filets
1 tsp. dillweed
⅛ tsp. salt
⅛ tsp. pepper
¾ cup leeks,
  thinly sliced
1 Tbsp. oil
4 cups green
  spinach leaves
Lemon wedges
Dillweed sprigs

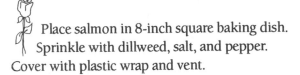 Place salmon in 8-inch square baking dish. Sprinkle with dillweed, salt, and pepper. Cover with plastic wrap and vent.

Microwave on HIGH for 4–5 minutes or until filets flake easily with fork.

In a small skillet, sauté leeks in oil until soft. Add spinach leaves and continue to cook until spinach is wilted.

Serve salmon filets on bed of spinach mixture; garnish with lemon wedges and dillweed sprigs.

SERVES: 2

Salmon on the Grill

4 large salmon steaks
½ cup soy sauce
2 Tbsp. brown sugar
¼ cup white wine
1 Tbsp. peanut oil

 Place salmon steaks in zippered plastic bag.

In a small bowl, combine the soy sauce, brown sugar, wine, and oil; mix well. Pour over salmon and marinate in the refrigerator several hours or overnight.

Remove salmon from marinade; reserve. Place salmon on grill over medium heat for 5–10 minutes.

In a saucepan, heat reserved marinade; ladle over salmon and serve.

SERVES: 4

Salmon With Red Pepper Sauce

2 medium-size sweet
  red peppers
2 Tbsp. butter
4 (6 oz.) salmon
  steaks, skinless
  and boneless
Salt and pepper
  to taste
4 Tbsp. shallots,
  finely chopped
¼ cup dry white wine
½ cup heavy cream
2 Tbsp. dill,
  finely chopped
Dill sprigs
  for garnish

 Core and remove seeds from red peppers. Cut into ¼-inch strips; set aside.

Heat butter in a non-stick skillet large enough to hold salmon steaks in one layer. Season both sides of steaks with salt and pepper. Place steaks in pan and cook over high heat until lightly brown, about 1½ minutes on each side. The time will vary depending on thickness of steak. Transfer steaks to warm platter.

Leave the cooking butter in skillet; add shallots and peppers. Cook, stirring until tender. Add wine and cook until reduced by half. Add cream; cook and stir over medium heat until reduced by half again. Taste for seasoning.

Add salmon steaks, chopped dill, and any juices that have accumulated around the steaks; bring to a simmer. Cook 1 minute. Do not overcook. Serve immediately with dill sprigs for decoration.

SERVES: 4

Salmon Oregon

4 fresh salmon
  steaks, 1-inch thick

5 Tbsp. frozen orange
  juice concentrate,
  thawed

⅓ cup water

⅓ cup soy sauce

2 tsp. fresh
  parsley, chopped

2 Tbsp. oil

½ tsp. garlic,
  finely chopped

1 tsp. dried
  basil, crushed

 Place steaks in shallow dish.

In a small bowl, combine orange juice, water, soy sauce, parsley, oil, garlic, and basil; mix well. Pour over salmon and let stand at room temperature for 1 hour or refrigerate 4–6 hours, turning occasionally in sauce.

Spray broiler pan with vegetable spray and place salmon on broiler pan, reserving marinade. Broil for 8 minutes per side or until cooked through.

In a small saucepan, heat remaining marinade to a boil. Reduce heat to medium and cook 5 minutes, stirring occasionally.

Place salmon on serving plate and ladle sauce over top.

SERVES: 4

Baked Salmon in Parchment

4 (6 oz.) salmon
  filets
4 sheets
  parchment paper
½ cup white wine
¼ cup olive oil
1 bunch leeks,
  thinly sliced
1 bunch fresh
  dill, divided
  Salt and pepper
  to taste
½ cup butter, melted
  Dill sprigs
  for garnish

 Place each filet in middle of parchment paper large enough to fold and enclose filet.

In a mixing bowl, combine wine and oil; pour over each filet in equal portions. Place leeks and dill sprigs next to filet and sprinkle with salt and pepper.

Brush edges of parchment paper with melted butter; fold to enclose fish. Brush outside of package with butter and place on baking sheet.

Bake at 350° for 10–15 minutes, until paper is puffy and brown.

To serve, remove paper and garnish filet with sprig of fresh dill.

NOTE: A wonderful entrée that goes well with Saffron Couscous.

SERVES: 4

Shrimp Scampi

2½ lbs. fresh shrimp, unpeeled
1 cup butter, melted
¼ cup olive oil
1 Tbsp. dried parsley flakes
1 Tbsp. lemon juice
¾ tsp. salt
¾ tsp. garlic powder
¾ tsp. dried basil
½ tsp. oregano

 Peel and devein shrimp; place in single layer in a 15x10x1-inch jelly roll pan.

In a mixing bowl, combine butter, oil, parsley flakes, lemon juice, salt, garlic powder, basil, and oregano; mix well. Pour over shrimp.

Bake at 450° for 5 minutes and then broil, 4 inches from heat, for 5 minutes or until shrimp are done.

NOTE: Serve over cooked rice.

SERVES: 6

Herbed Shrimp With Basil Mayonnaise

For the Shrimp:

2 lbs. shrimp, unpeeled

¾ cup olive oil

2 Tbsp. lemon juice

1 Tbsp. parsley, minced

2 garlic cloves, crushed

1 tsp. salt

½ tsp. dried oregano

Pepper to taste

Lemon slices for garnish

Parsley sprigs for garnish

For the Sauce:

2 cups fresh basil leaves

1 garlic clove, crushed

¼ tsp. salt

Pepper to taste

2 cups mayonnaise

 SHRIMP

Rinse shrimp and slit the underside of shell, but do not peel.

Combine remaining ingredients for marinade; set aside. Using six, 12-inch skewers, thread each shrimp at the wide end; then curl the shrimp into rounds and secure them through the tail ends.

Place skewered shrimp in a shallow dish. Pour marinade over shrimp and turn skewers to coat evenly. Let marinate for 2 hours, turning every 30 minutes.

Grill shrimp over hot coals for 3 minutes on each side, or until they are just cooked. Remove the shrimp from the skewers. Arrange in a bowl; garnish with lemon slices and parsley. Serve with basil mayonnaise sauce.

SAUCE

In a blender or food processor, process basil, garlic, salt, and pepper until finely minced. Add mayonnaise and pulse only until blended. Chill until ready to serve.

NOTE: May add small amount of lemon juice and salt to taste. May use fresh spinach instead of fresh basil.

SERVES: 4

Scallops and Vegetables With Sauce

For the Vegetables:

2 cups fresh
   mushrooms, sliced

1 cup green pepper,
   cut into chunks

¼ cup carrots,
   shredded

1 clove garlic,
   minced

3 Tbsp. margarine,
   divided

2 lbs. bay or sea
   scallops

Lemon wedge
   for garnish

Fresh dill sprig
   for garnish

For the Sauce:

1 (8 oz.) container
   soft cream cheese
   with chives and
   onion

¼ cup lowfat
   buttermilk

1 Tbsp. lemon juice

 VEGETABLES

In a large skillet, sauté vegetables and garlic in 2 tablespoons margarine over high heat for 3 minutes. Remove vegetables with slotted spoon. Reduce heat to low.

Sauté scallops in 1 tablespoon margarine in same skillet over low heat 6–8 minutes or until opaque; drain liquid.

Add vegetables to scallops in skillet; stir over low heat for 1 minute.

Serve with creamy chive and onion sauce. Garnish with lemon wedges and fresh dill sprig, if desired.

SAUCE

In a small sauce pan, stir together ingredients over low heat until smooth.

SERVES: 8

Lime Ginger Scallop Sauté

For the Scallops:

1 Tbsp. olive oil

1 Tbsp. butter

1 lb. sea scallops, patted dry

3 Tbsp. lime juice

⅓ cup walnut halves, lightly toasted

Parsley, chopped, for garnish

For the Butter:

4 Tbsp. butter, room temperature

2 tsp. grated lime zest

1 tsp. ground ginger

½ tsp. salt

Freshly ground pepper to taste

 SCALLOPS

In a large skillet, heat oil and butter over high heat. Add scallops and stir until golden, about 2 minutes. Pour off the fat.

Stir in lime juice and cook 1 minute. Lower heat and stir in lime ginger butter, 1 tablespoon at a time. Cook just until a thick sauce forms.

Stir in the walnuts. Sprinkle with parsley and serve.

BUTTER

In a small bowl, stir all ingredients until smooth.

SERVES: 2–4

Corn Crab Cakes

1 lb. fresh or frozen crabmeat

1 cup corn, cooked

½ cup onion, finely diced

½ cup green pepper, finely diced

½ cup celery, finely diced

1 cup mayonnaise

½ tsp. dry mustard

Cayenne pepper to taste

Salt and pepper to taste

1 egg, lightly beaten

1¼ cup cracker crumbs

2 Tbsp. olive oil or 2 Tbsp. butter

 In a large bowl, combine crabmeat, corn, onion, green pepper, and celery.

In another bowl, combine mayonnaise with mustard and cayenne pepper. Add to crabmeat mixture; season with salt and pepper.

Using a rubber spatula, gently fold egg and ¼ cup cracker crumbs into crab mixture.

Form crab mixture into eight patties.

Carefully coat patties with the remaining cracker crumbs. Chill, covered, for at least 30 minutes, but no longer than a few hours.

In a medium skillet, heat 1 tablespoon of butter or oil. Cook crab over medium heat until golden on both sides, about 3 minutes per side. Add more butter or oil as necessary.

Serve immediately, with tartar sauce on the side.

SERVES: 4

Tuna Ring Mold

2 (7 oz.) cans tuna

1 cup cracker crumbs

1 (10¾ oz.) can cream of celery soup

3 eggs, separated

2 Tbsp. parsley, chopped

2 Tbsp. pimiento, chopped

1 Tbsp. lemon juice

⅛ tsp. pepper

Parsley sprigs for garnish

In a large bowl, combine the tuna, cracker crumbs, soup, egg yolks, parsley, pimiento, lemon juice, and pepper.

In a small bowl, beat egg whites until stiff and fold into tuna mixture. Pour mixture into a well-greased ring mold.

Bake at 350° for 30 minutes. Unmold and serve; garnish with parsley sprigs.

NOTE: An attractive dish served with peas in center of tuna mold.

SERVES: 6

Filet of Sole Martinique

2 lbs. filet of sole

¾ tsp. garlic powder

1 (10¾ oz.) can cream of shrimp soup

2 Tbsp. cooking sherry

3 green onions, chopped

1 Tbsp. Parmesan cheese, grated

 Place filets in greased baking dish; sprinkle with garlic powder.

In a small bowl, combine the soup and sherry; pour over filets. Sprinkle onion and Parmesan on top.

Bake at 375° for 45 minutes or until fish flakes easily with fork.

SERVES: 4

French Fish Bake

1 egg yolk
¼ cup milk
½ cup seasoned
   bread crumbs
¼ tsp. salt
¼ tsp. pepper
1 Tbsp. parsley,
   chopped
1 Tbsp. onion,
   chopped
1 (7 oz.) can
   crabmeat
¼ cup butter, melted
   and divided
4 fish filets
½ cup sliced almonds

 Spread foil on baking dish and measure enough foil to make tent over fish; set aside.

In a bowl, combine egg yolk, milk, bread crumbs, salt, pepper, parsley, onions, crabmeat, and 2 tablespoons butter.

Place 2 filets in baking dish; spread crab mixture over filets and top with remaining filets. Brush with remaining butter and sprinkle with almonds. Fold foil loosely over fish.

Bake at 400° for 35 minutes. Uncover and bake 5 minutes to brown. Serve immediately.

NOTE: This recipe is excellent with bass, halibut, or red snapper.

SERVES: 2–4

Baked Rainbow Trout

2 Rainbow trout
Salt and pepper to taste
¼ cup flour
6 Tbsp. butter, divided
2 Tbsp. oil
½ lb. mushrooms, sliced
1 tsp. lemon juice
¾ cup scallions, sliced
¼ cup bread crumbs

 Salt and pepper trout; dust with flour.

In a skillet, melt 2 tablespoons butter and the oil; brown trout. Remove from pan and set aside.

Add 2 more tablespoons butter to skillet and sauté mushrooms; add lemon juice. Transfer mixture to buttered baking dish.

In same skillet, add remaining butter and sauté the scallions and bread crumbs.

Place trout on top of the mushroom mixture. Sprinkle onion mixture over trout.

Bake at 425°, uncovered, for 10 minutes or until done.

SERVES: 2–4

1907, Age 22

A Bess Recipe

Mrs. Truman's Turkey Stuffing

    10 slices dry bread
     1 cup diced onions
    ¼ pound butter
     1 cup diced celery
     1 cup hot water in which giblets have been cooked
        Salt, pepper, and poultry seasoning to taste

Dry out bread in slow oven. Cut into ½-inch cubes. Put butter in pan, add onions and celery and sauté until light brown. Add water and let simmer for 5 minutes. Add bread crumbs. Season with salt, pepper and poultry seasoning to taste.

Note: Dressing should be neither too wet nor too dry. It should be a semi-moist dressing so that when it is done it will be light and fluffy. This is an exceedingly fine dressing for chicken or turkey. For larger sized birds, the amounts must be increased accordingly.

Bess and Harry Truman spent Christmas, 1952, at the White House with the Wallace family and Harry's sister, Mary Jane Truman.

BELOW: Bess and Harry pose in front of the Christmas tree with the Wallaces and Mary Jane Truman for this family photo.

BOTTOM: The family gathers in the White House dining room.

Fancy Provolone Chicken

For the Chicken:

- 8 chicken breast halves
- 1 tsp. salt
- 2 egg whites
- 1 Tbsp. water
- 1 cup very fine bread crumbs
- 3 Tbsp. olive oil
- 4 oz. Provolone, shredded

For the Sauce:

- 3 Tbsp. butter
- 3 Tbsp. flour
- ¾ cup water
- ⅓ cup dry sherry
- ⅓ cup heavy cream
- 1 tsp. lemon juice
- 6 cloves garlic, minced
- ½ cup Shitake or other mushrooms, coarsely chopped
- ½ cup artichoke hearts, coarsely chopped
- ½ cup Asiago or Parmesan cheese, shredded
- ½ tsp. red pepper flakes
- ¼ tsp. freshly ground pepper
- ½ tsp. dried thyme

CHICKEN

Pound the thickest part of each breast so the thickness is fairly even. Sprinkle both sides with salt.

Whisk egg whites with water. Pour into flat dish. Put crumbs into another flat dish. Pour oil into bottom of large flat baking pan. Dip each breast, first into egg whites, turning to coat both sides, then into bread crumbs. Place in oiled baking pan. Bake at 350° for 20 minutes.

Remove pan from oven and raise temperature to 425°. Turn chicken over and top each breast with 2 tablespoons shredded Provolone. Pour sauce around the chicken. Bake additional 10 minutes. Transfer chicken to serving dish and pour sauce around, not over, chicken.

SAUCE

Heat butter in a medium sauce pan. Stir in flour and bring to a boil. Cook for 1 minute. Combine the liquid ingredients. Add to flour mixture and cook at a gentle boil for 1 minute. Remove from heat and add remaining ingredients.

NOTE: You may substitute olive oil for butter and milk for cream. Sauce may be made 3–4 days in advance and refrigerated, tightly covered.

SERVES: 8

Sherried Chicken Almondine

12 chicken breasts,
    boneless and
    skinless
½ tsp. salt
½ tsp. pepper
½ cup flour
¾ cup margarine
½ cup almonds, sliced
 2 (4 oz.) cans
    mushrooms, sliced,
    reserving liquid
½ cup sherry
½ cup of half & half

Salt and pepper chicken; dust with flour. Sauté chicken in margarine; brown each side. Begin with ½ cup margarine (add as needed). Remove chicken to baking dish.

Add sliced almonds to drippings and sauté 5 minutes, browning evenly; stir often.

Add mushrooms with their liquid; stir in sherry. Scrape bottom of pan to loosen drippings. Turn heat to low and slowly add half & half. Remove from heat as soon as blended.

Pour mixture over chicken. Bake, covered, at 350° for 45–50 minutes. Remove cover for last 10 minutes of baking.

NOTE: This can be frozen before baking.

SERVES: 10–12

Mediterranean Chicken

¾ lb. fresh
   mushrooms,
   thinly sliced

1 tsp. garlic, minced

¼ cup olive oil

4 whole chicken
   breasts, boneless
   and skinless, sliced
   into 8 strips
   Flour, seasoned, for
   dredging

2 oz. sun-dried
   tomatoes, chopped
   coarsely

¾ cup dry white wine

1 tsp. lemon rind,
   grated

¼ tsp. finis herbs,
   crumbled

In a large skillet, sauté mushrooms and garlic in a small amount of the olive oil for 1 minute. Transfer to plate.

Dredge chicken in flour and place in skillet; add oil as needed. Cook chicken until lightly brown. Transfer to plate.

Add tomatoes with wine and cook for 1 minute, scraping brown bits from bottom of skillet. Add mushrooms, lemon rind, and herbs; simmer 10 minutes. Add chicken to sauce; simmer on low heat 15 minutes or until ready to serve.

NOTE: Finis herbs are a mixture of dried chives, tarragon, chervil, parsley, and onions.

SERVES: 4

Chicken Royale

For the Stuffing:

2 cups dry bread crumbs

1 Tbsp. onion, chopped

½ tsp. salt

⅛ tsp. pepper

¼ tsp. poultry seasoning

¼ cup hot water

2 Tbsp. butter

For the Chicken:

4 small chicken breasts, whole

¼ cup flour

½ tsp. salt

⅛ tsp. pepper

¼ tsp. paprika

½ cup margarine, melted

Parsley, chopped, for garnish

For the Sauce:

½ lb. fresh mushrooms, cut in half

¼ cup onion, minced

2 Tbsp. margarine

2 Tbsp. flour

½ cup heavy cream

½ cup sour cream

½ tsp. salt

¼ tsp. pepper

 STUFFING

Mix all dry ingredients with hot water and butter; toss gently.

CHICKEN

Split whole chicken breasts, just enough to fold.

Combine flour, salt, pepper, and paprika in paper bag; add chicken and shake. Fill cavity of each piece with herb stuffing. Hold stuffing in by skewering opening of chicken with toothpicks.

Dip chicken in melted margarine; place in baking dish. (If any margarine remains, drizzle over top.)

Bake at 325° for 45 minutes; turn and bake an additional 45 minutes, or until tender. Sprinkle with parsley. Serve with mushroom sauce.

SAUCE

Cook mushrooms and onion in margarine until tender, but not brown. Cover and cook 10 minutes over low heat.

Push mushrooms to one side and stir flour into margarine. Add heavy cream, sour cream, salt, and pepper.

Heat slowly, stirring constantly, almost to boiling point.

SERVES: 4

Chicken Supreme

4 chicken breasts, whole

1 onion, chopped

1 carrot, sliced

2 stalks celery, cut

1 pkg. cornbread stuffing mix

½ cup margarine, melted

1 (10¾ oz.) can cream of chicken soup

1 (10½ oz.) can cream of mushroom soup

2 (14 oz.) cans chicken broth

1 (4 oz.) can mushrooms, drained

In a large stock pot, cover chicken breasts, onion, carrot, and celery with just enough water to cover; simmer slowly.

Toss stuffing mix with margarine. Reserve ¼ cup stuffing and put remainder in 9x13-inch oblong dish. Place cooked chicken breasts on stuffing mix. Mix soups, broth, and drained mushrooms. Pour over chicken. Top with reserved stuffing mix.

Bake, uncovered, at 350° for 45–60 minutes.

SERVES: 4–6

Mandarin Florentine Chicken

6 large chicken breast halves, boneless and skinless

For the Stuffing:

¾ cup cooked orzo (pasta)

1 cup frozen cut leaf spinach, thawed and drained

1 (11 oz.) can mandarin orange segments, drained, reserving liquid

⅓ cup onion, chopped

1 clove garlic, crushed

Salt and pepper to taste

For the Sauce:

⅔ cup orange juice

⅔ cup reserved mandarin orange liquid

1 Tbsp. cornstarch

2 tsp. fresh tarragon, chopped or ¾ tsp. dried tarragon

½ tsp. salt

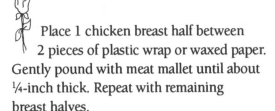 Place 1 chicken breast half between 2 pieces of plastic wrap or waxed paper. Gently pound with meat mallet until about ¼-inch thick. Repeat with remaining breast halves.

STUFFING

In a medium bowl, combine stuffing ingredients; mix well. Place ⅓ cup of stuffing mixture in center of each chicken breast. Bring ends of breasts over stuffing; fold in sides. Secure with wooden picks. Place stuffed chicken breasts seam side down in ungreased 9x13-inch baking dish; set aside.

SAUCE

In a small saucepan, combine sauce ingredients; blend well. Bring to a boil over medium-high heat. Cook 3–5 minutes until sauce is thickened, stirring constantly; pour over chicken.

Bake at 350° for 45–50 minutes or until chicken is fork-tender and juices run clear. Garnish with additional mandarin oranges and fresh tarragon, if desired.

NOTE: Orzo is a rice-shaped pasta sometimes called rosamarina (⅓–½ cup uncooked orzo will yield ¾ cup).

SERVES: 6

Fantastic Chicken

1 (8 oz.) jar
  apricot preserves
1 (8 oz.) bottle
  Russian dressing
1 pkg. onion
  soup mix
6 chicken breasts,
  boneless and
  skinless

 In a bowl, mix apricot preserves, dressing, and soup mix. Place the chicken breasts in a large oven proof baking dish and pour apricot mixture over chicken.

Bake, uncovered, at 300° for 1–1½ hours.

SERVES: 6

Chicken With Almonds

4 chicken breasts,
  boneless and
  skinless
¼ cup flour
½ tsp. salt
½ tsp. pepper
8 Tbsp. butter,
  divided
2 Tbsp. lemon juice
  Additional salt
  and pepper
1 cup almonds,
  whole
1 tsp. fresh garlic,
  minced
1 Tbsp. onion,
  chopped
¼ cup dry white wine
2 tsp. chopped,
  parsley, optional

Cook chicken breasts in boiling water for 2 minutes. Drain and pat dry.

Mix flour, salt, and pepper. Dredge the breasts in flour mixture. In a large skillet, melt 4 tablespoons of butter. Brown chicken breasts on both sides. Add lemon juice; salt and pepper, to taste.

Cover and cook until tender, approximately 5 minutes. Remove from pan.

Add to the skillet 2 tablespoons butter, almonds, garlic, and onion; shake over heat until almonds brown. Stir in remaining butter, wine, and parsley. Return chicken to skillet; reheat.

SERVES: 4

Poppy Seed Chicken

½ cup flour
½ tsp. salt
⅛ tsp. pepper
1¼ cups butter, divided
8 chicken breasts
2 (10¾ oz.) cans cream of chicken soup
1 (16 oz.) carton sour cream
1 Tbsp. poppy seeds
2 cups Ritz crackers, crushed

Mix flour, salt, and pepper. Melt ½ cup butter in large baking pan. Dredge chicken in flour mixture. Dip both sides of chicken in butter and place skin side down in pan.

Bake at 375° for 1 hour. Cool. Remove chicken from bone, leaving on the crispy skin.

Place meat in 9x13-inch casserole dish. Combine soup and sour cream; pour over chicken. Combine poppy seeds, cracker crumbs, and ¾ cup melted butter. Spread over soup mixture.

Bake at 350° for 30 minutes or until bubbly.

SERVES: 8

Zesty Grilled Chicken

8 chicken breasts,
  halved, boneless
  and skinless
¼ cup olive oil or
  canola oil
¼ cup soy sauce
2 Tbsp. lemon juice
1 Tbsp. brown sugar
2 cloves garlic,
  minced
3 whole cloves
  Dash pepper
½ tsp. dried thyme
½ tsp. dried basil

 Place chicken breasts in a glass dish.

Prepare marinade with remaining ingredients. Pour marinade over chicken and refrigerate a minimum of 4 hours. May be refrigerated up to 24 hours.

Grill quickly over hot coals, basting frequently.

NOTE: Fresh herbs may be used. Substitute 2 teaspoons fresh for ½ teaspoon dried.

SERVES: 4–6

Grilled Chicken With Bacon

3 whole chicken
  breasts, split,
  boneless and
  skinless
3 oz. cream cheese
1 cup mushrooms,
  thinly sliced
½ cup green onion,
  chopped
12 strips bacon

Place each chicken breast between 2 pieces of wax paper and pound to ½-inch thickness.

Dab cream cheese on top of pounded chicken breast. Add mushrooms and onions. Roll chicken and then wrap with 2 slices of bacon. Secure with several toothpicks.

Grill on medium-high over drip pan; use tongs to turn. Grill 3–4 minutes on each side. Bacon will be crispy and chicken will be tender inside.

SERVES: 4–6

Skewered Chicken

3 medium chicken
  breasts, split,
  boneless and
  skinless

¼ cup tamari or low-
  sodium soy sauce

3 Tbsp. dry
  white wine

2 Tbsp. lemon juice

2 Tbsp. cooking oil

¾ tsp. Italian
  seasoning spice

½ tsp. grated
  ginger root

1 clove garlic,
  minced

¼ tsp. onion powder

⅛ tsp. pepper

Cut chicken into 1¼-inch strips. Thread loosely onto 6–8 metal skewers. Place in shallow baking dish.

Combine marinade ingredients. Pour over chicken. Cover and chill 2–3 hours.

Grill over hot coals 3–4 minutes per side. (Grill on high for gas grill.)

NOTE: Chicken strips may be marinated in large bowl and put on skewer before grilling. (This takes up less refrigerator space.)

SERVES: 4–6

Honey Mustard Chicken Bake or Kabobs

For the Sauce:
- ½ cup butter
- ½ cup honey
- ¼ cup Dijon mustard
- ½ tsp. salt
- ½ tsp. pepper

For the Kabobs:
- 24 large mushrooms, fresh
- 1½ lbs. chicken breasts, boneless and skinless, cut into 1½-inch pieces
- 24 red pepper pieces, cut into 1½-inch pieces
- 24 wedges pineapple, fresh
- 24 zucchini slices, 1-inch thick

For the Chicken:
- 1 (3 lb.) chicken, cut up

SAUCE

Melt butter in small saucepan. Whisk in the honey, mustard, salt, and pepper.

NOTE: Honey mustard sauce may be used for grilled kabobs or for oven-baked chicken.

KABOBS

Thread long metal skewers with mushrooms, 3 pieces chicken, red pepper, pineapple wedge, and zucchini. Repeat. Brush kabobs generously with sauce.

Grill 6 inches above medium, indirect heat for 15–20 minutes; turn once and baste frequently with sauce. Serve remaining sauce on the side, to be spooned over kabobs as desired.

YIELD: 12 kabobs

CHICKEN

Place chicken in a 9x13-inch baking dish. Spread sauce over chicken.

Bake at 350° for 1 hour, basting with the pan juices every 15 minutes until done.

SERVES: 4

Chicken Over the Coals

2 fryers (2½ lbs.
  each), cut-up
2 Tbsp. apple jelly
¼ cup salad oil
¼ cup white wine
¼ cup chicken broth
2 Tbsp. lemon juice
¼ tsp. garlic salt
1 tsp. salt
1 Tbsp. parsley,
  snipped
½ tsp. prepared
  mustard
½ tsp. Worcestershire
  sauce
½ tsp. celery seed
½ tsp. rosemary
½ tsp. pepper

Stir jelly until thinned and smooth. Add remaining ingredients for sauce. Brush chicken with sauce and let stand 30 minutes at room temperature.

Grill over indirect heat about 1 hour, turning and basting about every 15 minutes. Meat should be tender and skin crisp when done.

SERVES: 8

Chicken Breast Wellington

For the Chicken:

6 whole chicken breasts, boned and split

Seasoned salt and pepper, to taste

1 (6 oz.) pkg. wild rice, prepared according to package directions

¼ cup grated orange peel

2 eggs, separated

3 (8 oz.) cans refrigerated crescent rolls

1 Tbsp. water

For the Sauce:

2 (10 oz.) jars currant jelly

1 Tbsp. prepared mustard

3 Tbsp. port wine

¼ cup lemon juice

CHICKEN

Flatten chicken breast; sprinkle with seasoned salt and pepper. Cook rice according to package directions; add orange peel. Cool. Beat egg whites until soft peaks form and fold into rice.

On floured surface, roll 2 triangular pieces of crescent rolls, closing perforations. Place flattened chicken breast on flat surface. Spoon ¼ cup rice mixture on chicken and roll up. Place chicken roll in center of prepared crescent dough. Bring dough over stuffed breast. Moisten edges of dough with water and press to seal together. Place seam side down in greased baking dish. Beat egg yolks slightly with water; brush over dough.

Bake, uncovered, at 375° for 45–50 minutes, until breasts are tender.

SAUCE

Heat currant jelly; gradually stir in mustard, wine, and lemon juice. Serve with chicken as a sauce.

NOTE: If you prefer a thicker sauce, add 1 tablespoon cornstarch and stir into sauce.

- You can cut leaves or flowers out of dough to decorate top of Chicken Wellington. Place on wrapped chicken roll and brush with egg before baking.

SERVES: 12

Chicken in Sour Cream

1 (3 lb.) chicken,
  cut-up
½ cup flour
  Seasoned salt
  to taste
⅔ cup water
1 (12 oz.) carton
  sour cream
2 tsp. onion, minced
½ tsp. salt
¼ tsp. pepper

Dredge pieces of chicken in flour and seasoned salt. Place in greased baking pan and add water; cover.

Bake at 350° for 30 minutes. Reduce heat to 325°. Mix sour cream, onion, salt, and pepper. Pour over chicken; bake, uncovered, 1 hour longer.

NOTE: This recipe goes especially well with Easy Browned Rice (see page 260).

SERVES: 4–6

Roast Chicken With Lemon

1 (2½ lb.) chicken, whole
Salt and pepper to taste
2 lemons, whole

Wash chicken thoroughly. Drain all water out of cavity. Dry it well with paper towels. Sprinkle liberally with salt and pepper, inside and out.

Rinse lemons and soften by rolling between palms of your hands or placing in microwave for 10 seconds. Prick each lemon with toothpick at least 20 times. Place both lemons in cavity of chicken and lace closed with skewer.

Put chicken in a roasting pan, breast side down; place in the upper third of oven. Bake at 350° for 20 minutes.

Turn chicken, with the breast side facing up. Bake for an additional 25 minutes. Turn heat up to 400° and bake another 20 minutes, or until juices run clear. Discard lemons and slice chicken to serve.

NOTE: This recipe has no fat and is self-basting. A quick and easy way to serve chicken.

SERVES: 4

Hot Mama Casserole

2 lbs. chicken
   breasts, boneless
   and skinless,
   cooked and cooled

Butter-flavored
   cooking spray

1 can cream of
   chicken soup

1 cup light sour
   cream

1 Tbsp. chili powder

1 tsp. ground cumin

12 corn tortillas

1 (2½ oz.) can
   green chiles

½ cup onion, chopped

2 cups sharp
   Cheddar cheese,
   shredded

1 (10 oz.) can diced
   tomatoes and green
   chiles

 Cut cooked chicken into bite-size cubes.

Spray 3-quart casserole dish with butter-flavored cooking spray. On medium heat, mix cream of chicken soup, sour cream, chili powder, and cumin.

Line casserole with tortillas that have been dipped in soup mixture. Layer chicken, green chiles, onion, and cheese. Repeat layers, ending with cheese.

Top casserole with the can of tomatoes and green chiles.

Bake at 350° for 45 minutes. Cool 10 minutes.

SERVES: 6

Chicken and Spaghetti Provencale

4 cups canned
  stewed tomatoes

2 cups chicken broth

1 Tbsp. parsley,
  chopped

1 large onion, cut
  into quarters

1 clove garlic,
  minced

1 Tbsp.
  Worcestershire
  sauce

2 tsp. salt

½ tsp. basil

½ tsp. thyme

1 lb. fresh
  mushrooms, sliced

2 Tbsp. butter

4 cups chicken,
  cooked, cut into
  bite-size pieces

2 Tbsp. flour

1 cup light cream

½ lb. Cheddar cheese,
  grated and divided

Salt and pepper
  to taste

½ lb. spaghetti

Simmer canned tomatoes and chicken broth until liquid is reduced by one-half. Season broth with next 7 ingredients.

In a large skillet, sauté sliced mushrooms in butter until golden. With a slotted spoon, transfer mushrooms to broth mixture along with cooked chicken.

Stir 2 tablespoons flour into mushroom drippings; add light cream and half the Cheddar cheese. Heat and stir until thickened. Season to taste with salt and pepper. Add to broth mixture.

Cook spaghetti according to package directions and toss with sauce.

Turn mixture into an 8x10-inch casserole dish. Sprinkle top with remaining Cheddar cheese.

Bake at 350° for 45 minutes or until bubbly.

NOTE: The casserole may be frozen.

SERVES: 8

Crescent Chicken Casserole

3 cups chicken, cooked and diced

1 (4 oz.) can mushrooms

½ cup sliced water chestnuts

1 can cream of chicken or mushroom soup

½ cup white wine

⅔ cup mayonnaise

½ cup celery, chopped

¼ cup onion, chopped

½ cup sour cream

1 (8 oz.) can crescent rolls or biscuits

2 Tbsp. butter

⅔ cup Swiss cheese, shredded

½ cup almonds, slivered

In a sauce pan, combine first 9 ingredients. Stir over medium heat until mixture is hot and bubbly.

Pour into ungreased 9x13-inch baking dish. Separate crescent rolls or biscuits; place over hot chicken mixture. Brush with the butter. Top with Swiss cheese and almonds.

Bake at 375° for 25 minutes or until crust is brown.

NOTE: When using biscuits, bake mixture about 10 minutes before adding the biscuits and toppings. Bake for the remaining 15 minutes.

SERVES: 6–8

Chicken Divan

2 (10 oz.) pkgs. frozen broccoli spears

3 cups cooked chicken, cubed

2 cans cream of chicken soup

1 cup mayonnaise

1 Tbsp. lemon juice

½ cup bread crumbs

¼ cup butter, melted

½ cup sharp Cheddar cheese, grated

Cook broccoli until tender. Arrange drained broccoli in a 2-quart greased casserole. Top with cubed chicken and cover with the combined soup, mayonnaise, and lemon juice. Combine the melted butter and bread crumbs. Spread grated cheese on top and sprinkle with bread crumb mixture.

Bake at 325° for 45 minutes.

NOTE: Can use 1 cup packaged cornbread dressing mix on top.

SERVES: 6

Microwave Oriental Chicken Breasts

For the Chicken:

¼ cup celery, minced

½ cup onion, minced

1 (8 oz.) can water chestnuts, well-drained, minced

1 lb. lean pork sausage

¼ cup milk

1 cup bread crumbs

1 egg

1 Tbsp. Teriyaki sauce

½ tsp. ground ginger

2 drops hot sauce

6 whole chicken breasts, boneless and skinless

Sesame seeds

For the Sauce:

¼ cup butter

¼ cup honey

2 Tbsp. soy sauce

1 tsp. cornstarch

 CHICKEN

Using a non-metal colander, sitting in 2-quart glass dish, combine celery, onion, water chestnuts, and sausage. Microwave on HIGH for 4 minutes, stirring once. Pour off drippings.

Blend with milk, bread crumbs, egg, Teriyaki sauce, ginger, and hot sauce.

Flatten chicken breasts. Divide mixture and spread on chicken. Roll and secure with toothpick.

SAUCE

Mix all ingredients and boil until thickened. Pour over chicken in 8x12-inch glass dish. Sprinkle with sesame seeds.

Microwave on HIGH, covered, 25–30 minutes; rotate dish ¼-turn and baste halfway through cooking. Rest, covered, for 5 minutes.

Serve with rice.

NOTE: A yummy dish to serve guests. Prepare in quantity for a crowd.

SERVES: 6–8

Moo Goo Gai Pan

For the Chicken:

¼ cup peanut oil

½ lb. chicken, cut into pieces

¼ lb. fresh snow peas

1 (8 oz.) can bamboo shoots, drained

2 cups napa cabbage, sliced

½ cup mushrooms, sliced

½ cup water chestnuts, sliced

1 tsp. salt

½ cup chicken stock

For the Sauce:

2 Tbsp. cornstarch mixed with ¼ cup water

1 Tbsp. soy sauce

1 Tbsp. sherry

2 Tbsp. sugar

Dash sesame oil

CHICKEN

Stir-fry chicken in hot peanut oil for 30–45 seconds; add vegetables and salt. Stir-fry about 10–30 seconds.

Add chicken stock; bring to a boil. Cover and steam 1–3 minutes.

SAUCE

Combine sauce ingredients and stir into hot mixture. Mix thoroughly, adding sesame oil.

Serve over rice.

SERVES: 4

Chicken Pita Pockets

6 medium chicken
  breast halves,
  boneless and
  skinless (about
  1¾ lbs.)
3 Tbsp. olive or
  salad oil
1 tsp. dried oregano
1½ tsp. salt, divided
1 medium cucumber
1 (8 oz.) carton plain
  low-fat yogurt
1 garlic clove, minced
6 (6- to 8-inch) pitas
1 cup onion,
  thinly sliced
1 cup lettuce,
  thinly sliced
1 medium
  tomato, diced

Cut chicken breasts into 1-inch chunks. Toss chicken with oil, oregano and 1 teaspoon salt; set aside.

Peel cucumber, cut in half lengthwise; scrape out seeds. Coarsely shred cucumber onto paper towels. Roll and press to remove as much liquid as possible.

Mix cucumber, yogurt, garlic, and ½ teaspoon salt; set aside.

Wrap pitas in foil. Warm in 300° oven.

In a large skillet, cook chicken over medium heat, browning on both sides until done. Remove from skillet with slotted spoon. Keep warm.

In drippings, cook onion until tender, about 5 minutes.

To serve, spread cucumber mixture on warm pitas; top with sliced lettuce, chicken, onion, and tomato.

SERVES: 6

Herbed Turkey

1 (16–18 lb.) turkey
2 Tbsp. salt
1 Tbsp. fresh ginger
   root, grated
1 tsp. cumin seeds
½ cup butter, melted
1 bay leaf
1½ tsp. fresh tarragon
   (½ tsp. dried)
1½ tsp. fresh rosemary
   (½ tsp. dried)
1½ tsp. fresh dillweed
   (½ tsp. dried)
1 Tbsp. honey
1 Tbsp. A-1 Sauce
½ cup dry Sherry
1 cooking bag

 Remove giblets and neck from turkey. Rinse with cold water; pat dry.

In a mortar, crush together salt, ginger root, and cumin seeds. Rub cavity and skin of turkey with this mixture. Wrap turkey securely in a large plastic bag and refrigerate overnight.

Add herbs to hot butter and let set at room temperature overnight. Keep the butter mixture soft, but not melted. When ready to bake, work herbed butter under the skin of the turkey and in the cavity. Tie end of legs to tail with cord; tuck wing tips under breast. Combine honey, A-1 Sauce, and sherry; brush over turkey.

Place in cooking bag and bake according to directions on bag.

NOTE: May also be grilled or smoked.

SERVES: 8–12

Cornish Hens With Lemon and Rosemary

6 Cornish game
   hens, split
¾ cup lemon juice
½ cup olive oil
   Garlic salt
   Lemon pepper
   Rosemary

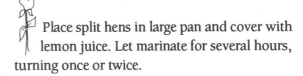 Place split hens in large pan and cover with lemon juice. Let marinate for several hours, turning once or twice.

Drain juice. Spray a broiler pan with cooking spray. Brush hens with olive oil; season both sides with garlic salt, lemon pepper, and rosemary, to taste.

Bake at 350° for 30–35 minutes. Increase heat to 425° for 5 minutes or place under broiler until skin is brown.

NOTE: These hens may also be broiled or grilled.

SERVES: 8–12

1917, Age 32

Mrs. Truman's Tuna and Noodle Casserole

1 7-ounce can of tuna fish, drained
½ package of egg noodles
   Boiling salted water
   Dabs of butter
   Hard cooked egg and parsley (for garnish)

White Cheese Sauce

2 tablespoons butter
1½ cups milk
¼ teaspoon salt
⅛ teaspoon pepper
¼ pound sharp cheddar cheese, grated
   Flour (to thicken)

Boil the noodles in boiling salted water for 12 minutes, or until tender. Drain well. Drain the tuna, and flake with a fork.

Make the cheese sauce as follows: Over low heat, melt the butter, and blend in the flour, stirring constantly until smooth. Gradually add the milk, continuing to stir constantly until the boiling point is reached. Now add the grated cheddar cheese, and the seasonings, to taste. Reduce heat and cook for 3 minutes longer, stirring all the while.

Into a well-buttered casserole put alternate layers of the boiled noodles and the tuna, covering it all with the cheese sauce. Dab generously with dabs of butter. Bake in a moderate oven (375°F) for 30 minutes. Garnish with sliced hard boiled egg or eggs, and sprigs of parsley.

ABOVE: Bess Truman had a love of knowledge. In this photo from the early 1900s, she is pictured reading on the back steps of 219 North Delaware as her brother, Frank, relaxes nearby.

Pesto Salad

For the Sauce:

3 Tbsp. pine nuts, toasted

2 cups fresh basil

2 cloves garlic, lightly crushed

1 tsp. salt

½ cup olive oil

3 Tbsp. butter, softened

¾ cup Parmesan cheese, grated

For the Salad:

1 red pepper, cut into ½-inch pieces

8 oz. rotelle noodles

1 cup pesto (recipe above)

1 (10 oz.) pkg. frozen peas, slightly thawed

1 (7 oz.) can light tuna or chicken, drained

Salt and pepper to taste

 SAUCE

Toast pine nuts on cookie sheet at 350° until brown. Place basil leaves, nuts, garlic, and salt in blender or food processor. Turn processor on and begin adding the oil through the feed tube. Blend until well-combined. Scrape down the sides, if necessary, and mix again.

Lightly mix in the softened butter and grated Parmesan cheese. The sauce should be thin enough to run off the spatula easily. If it seems too thick, blend in a little more oil.

NOTE: If fresh basil is unavailable, substitute 2 cups spinach leaves and 2 teaspoons dried basil.

SALAD

In a saucepan of boiling water, blanch cut red pepper for 30 seconds. Drain in a colander and refresh the pepper under running cold water. Drain well.

Cook pasta according to package directions, until al denté. Drain well.

In a large bowl, combine the pasta with pesto sauce, peas, tuna, and red peppers; salt and pepper. Chill, covered, for at least 1 hour or overnight.

Serve at room temperature.

SERVES: 6

Pasta Salad Allegro

For the Dressing:

- 1 large garlic clove, peeled
- 2 Tbsp. Balsamic or wine vinegar
- 1 Tbsp. fresh basil, finely cut
- ½ tsp. salt
- ¼ tsp. dried oregano
  Pepper to taste
- ¼ cup salad oil
- 2 Tbsp. olive oil

For the Salad:

- 8 oz. spinach pasta
- 4 oz. Provolone cheese, chilled in freezer 1 hour
- 6 oz. pepperoni, rind removed
- 1 medium zucchini
- ½ large red sweet pepper, cut into strips
- ½ large green pepper, cut into strips
- 1 small red onion, chopped
- 1 medium tomato, finely chopped
- 14 jumbo pitted black olives, sliced
- ½ cup loosely packed parsley, chopped

 DRESSING

Place all ingredients except oils in food processor and mix well. Add oils in a small stream until combined; refrigerate.

YIELD: ½ cup

SALAD

Cook pasta according to package directions. Drain well and set aside.

Shred cheese and set aside. Slice pepperoni into thin slices; stack pieces and cut into thin strips. Combine meat and prepared vegetables with pasta. Pour dressing over and toss well. Add parsley and toss.

Sprinkle with Provolone cheese and serve at room temperature.

SERVES: 6

Garden Pasta

½ cup parsley,
  finely chopped

2 garlic cloves,
  minced

1 cup onion, minced

6 slices Prosciutto,
  minced

4 radishes, minced

2 carrots, minced

1 large leek, minced
  (mostly white,
  some green tops)

⅓ cup fresh basil,
  minced, or 1 tsp.
  dried basil

3 Tbsp. butter

3 Tbsp. olive oil

1 cup cabbage, finely
  chopped

4 tomatoes, peeled
  and diced

2 small zucchini,
  diced

1 cup chicken broth

Salt and pepper
  to taste

12 oz. favorite pasta,
  cooked, and
  buttered

Parmesan cheese,
  freshly grated

 Combine parsley, garlic, onion, Prosciutto, radishes, carrots, leek, and basil.

In a large pot, heat butter and oil; stir in minced vegetable mixture. Simmer until onions and carrots are soft. Stir in cabbage, tomatoes, zucchini, and chicken broth. Season with salt and pepper; simmer, covered, for 20 minutes.

Serve with hot buttered pasta, lavished with freshly grated cheese.

SERVES: 6–8

Penne With Tomato Cream Sauce

1 Tbsp. butter

1 Tbsp. olive oil

1 small onion, chopped

1 (28 oz.) can Italian plum tomatoes, drained, seeded, and chopped

1 cup whipping cream

¼ cup vodka, optional

¼ tsp. dried crushed red pepper

Salt and pepper to taste

1 lb. penne pasta

Parmesan cheese, freshly grated

Fresh chives, minced

In a large, heavy saucepan, melt butter with oil over medium heat. Add onion and sauté until translucent. Add tomatoes, cooking until almost no liquid remains in pan, stirring frequently. Add cream, vodka, and red pepper; boil until thickened to sauce consistency. Season to taste with salt and pepper.

Cook pasta according to package directions, until al denté; drain well. Transfer to large bowl.

Bring sauce to a simmer; pour over pasta and toss well. Sprinkle with Parmesan and chives.

NOTE: Sauce can be prepared 1 day ahead. Cover and refrigerate.

SERVES: 4

Beef and Red Pepper Penne

2 Tbsp. cornstarch
¼ cup soy sauce
1½ cups beef broth
2 Tbsp. Scotch
1 Tbsp. sugar
1 tsp. Asian (toasted) sesame oil
3 Tbsp. vegetable oil
1 lb. boneless sirloin, cut into ¼-inch strips
2 red bell peppers, cut into julienne strips
2 large garlic cloves, minced
2 Tbsp. fresh ginger root, minced
6 scallions, sliced thin diagonally
1 tsp. dried hot red pepper flakes
Salt to taste
1 lb. penne pasta

In a bowl, whisk together the cornstarch, soy sauce, broth, Scotch, sugar, and sesame oil; set aside.

In a large heavy skillet or wok, heat 1 tablespoon vegetable oil over high heat until it just begins to smoke. Pat beef dry and add to oil in 2 batches, cooking for 30 seconds. Brown until center of meat is still pink. Using a slotted spoon, transfer beef, as it browns, to a bowl.

In the skillet, heat 1 tablespoon vegetable oil over moderately high heat until it is hot, but not smoking. Stir-fry the bell peppers for 2 minutes, or until they are crisp-tender. Remove and add to beef.

In the remaining tablespoon of vegetable oil, stir-fry the garlic and the ginger root over moderately high heat for 30 seconds. Stir the cornstarch mixture and add it to the skillet. Cook the sauce, stirring until it is thickened. Stir in the beef mixture, scallions, red pepper flakes; salt to taste.

Cook pasta according to package directions, until al denté; drain well. In a large bowl, toss pasta with the beef mixture.

SERVES: 4–6

Spinach Pasta With Gorgonzola

¼ lb. imported
   Gorgonzola cheese,
   crumbled
½ cup milk
3 Tbsp. butter
⅓ cup heavy cream
1 lb. spinach pasta
½ cup fresh Parmesan
   cheese, grated

Combine the Gorgonzola, milk, and butter in a large, non-aluminum skillet. Place over low heat and stir until the sauce is hot and well-blended.

Add the cream; stir until sauce is hot and well-blended.

Cook pasta according to package directions, until al denté; drain well. Toss with sauce and Parmesan until evenly coated.

Serve immediately.

NOTE: This sauce may be made ahead and reheated at serving time.

SERVES: 6–8

Smittellini Tortellini

2 (9 oz.) pkgs.
  refrigerated
  sausage-stuffed
  tortellini
4 Tbsp. margarine
3 oz. Prosciutto, cut
  into strips
2 cups half & half
1 cup whipping
  cream
½ tsp. pepper
½ tsp. garlic salt
2 egg yolks
4 Tbsp. Parmesan
  cheese, shredded

Cook tortellini according to package directions until just tender. Drain and keep warm.

In a 10-inch skillet, melt margarine; add the Prosciutto, and cook for 1 minute. Add the half & half and cream. Bring to boil and cook uncovered for 5 minutes or until slightly thickened; stir occasionally. Stir pepper and garlic salt into the cream sauce.

Slightly beat the egg yolks. Gradually add ¾ cup of the hot cream sauce into the egg yolks. Return egg mixture to the skillet; cook and stir about 2 minutes. Add the tortellini to the cream mixture and toss to coat. Transfer to a serving bowl. Sprinkle with Parmesan.

NOTE: May use ⅔ cup of any fully cooked ham instead of Prosciutto. May also serve extra Parmesan cheese.

SERVES: 4

Ham With Asparagus Pasta

1 lb. fettucine
1½ lbs. fresh
  asparagus
1 tsp. salt
6 oz. boiled
  unsmoked ham, cut
  into ¼-inch strips
2 Tbsp. butter,
  divided
1 cup heavy cream
⅔ cup Parmesan
  cheese, freshly
  grated
  Salt to taste

Cook fettucine according to package directions, until al denté. Drain well and transfer to a warm serving bowl.

Wash asparagus in cold water, cutting off tough ends. Place asparagus in 2 inches boiling water with 1 teaspoon salt in covered pan. Cook 4–8 minutes or until tender, but firm; drain.

Sauté ham strips in 1 tablespoon butter. Cook gently over medium heat for 2–3 minutes. Do not crisp ham. Remove and reserve. Melt 1 tablespoon butter in pan; add asparagus and turn to coat.

Add the ham to the asparagus. Add cream and turn the heat to medium-high. Stir constantly about 30 seconds or until the cream thickens. Remove from heat; salt.

Combine the fettucine and cream sauce. Toss thoroughly; add ⅔ cup Parmesan. Serve immediately.

SERVES: 6

Spaghetti With Red Peppers

6 Tbsp. olive oil

2 Tbsp. garlic, minced

2 large, sweet red peppers, cut lengthwise into ¼-inch strips

4 cups canned Italian tomatoes

1 tsp. oregano

6 whole fresh basil leaves or dried basil to taste

Salt and freshly ground pepper to taste

¼ cup dry white wine

8 oz. spaghetti

Heat oil in a skillet and add the garlic. Cook briefly and when garlic starts to turn brown, add the pepper strips. Cook over high heat, stirring constantly, about 5 minutes.

Put the tomatoes in saucepan. Add oregano and basil; salt and pepper. Bring to a boil and cook about 10 minutes. Add the pepper strips and wine. Cook about 10 minutes, stirring often. Serve over spaghetti. Garnish with fresh basil leaves.

Cook spaghetti according to package directions; drain well. Pour sauce over spaghetti and garnish with basil leaves.

SERVES: 4

Swedish Spaghetti

8 oz. bacon, cut in
½-inch pieces

1 cup onion, chopped

1 (8 oz.) can
tomato sauce

1 (14½ oz.) can
whole, peeled
tomatoes,
undrained

½ tsp. parsley flakes

1 tsp. Italian
seasoning

½ tsp. basil

½ tsp. garlic powder

½ tsp. sugar

Salt and pepper
to taste

8 oz. thin spaghetti
or vermicelli

Parmesan cheese

In a large skillet, cook bacon on medium heat for 5 minutes; drain grease. Add onions and cook until transparent. Add tomato sauce, tomatoes, parsley flakes, seasonings, and sugar. Simmer for 20–30 minutes to blend flavors.

Cook pasta according to package directions; drain well. Return drained pasta to pot; add sauce and mix together.

Garnish with shredded Parmesan, if desired.

SERVES: 4

Baked Spaghetti

1 lb. ground beef
1 cup onion, diced
1 Tbsp. chili powder
1 (6 oz.) can tomato paste
1 qt. water
8 oz. spaghetti
1 (6 oz.) can mushrooms, chopped
1 (10 oz.) can ripe olives, chopped
Pimiento, optional
1 (10 oz.) can whole kernel corn, undrained
1 cup Cheddar cheese, grated

In a large pan, brown ground beef and onion. Add chili powder, tomato paste, and water; bring to a boil. Add next 5 ingredients. Place in a greased 2-quart baking dish. Sprinkle top with grated cheese. Bake, covered, at 350° for 30–35 minutes. Uncover and bake additional 15 minutes.

NOTE: A quick and easy dish that kids love!

SERVES: 6

Spaghetti Sauce With Meatballs

For the Meatballs:

8 slices bread

2 lbs. ground beef

4 eggs

1 cup Parmesan or Romano cheese, grated

¼ cup parsley, snipped

2 cloves garlic, minced

1 tsp. oregano

2 tsp. salt

⅛ tsp. pepper

4 Tbsp. olive oil

For the Sauce:

1½ cups onion, chopped

2 cloves garlic, minced

⅓ cup olive or salad oil

2 (28 oz.) cans tomatoes

4 (6 oz.) cans `tomato paste

2 cups water

2 Tbsp. sugar

1 Tbsp. salt

½ tsp. pepper

1 Tbsp. oregano, crushed

2 bay leaves

1 recipe Meatballs

 MEATBALLS

Soak bread in water 2–3 minutes, then squeeze out moisture. Combine soaked bread with ground beef, eggs, Parmesan or Romano cheese, parsley, garlic, oregano, salt, and pepper; mix well. Form in small balls (about 40).

In a skillet, brown slowly in hot oil or place meatballs on oven broiler pan and bake at 350° for 30 minutes, or until browned.

SAUCE

Cook onion and garlic in hot oil until tender, but not brown. Stir in the next 8 ingredients. Simmer uncovered, for 30 minutes, stirring occasionally. Remove bay leaves.

Add meatballs; continue cooking about 30 minutes before serving.

NOTE: Sauce is excellent for freezing. Ladle cooled sauce into jars or freezer containers, allowing a little space at top of each. Freeze immediately. Heat to serve.

YIELD: 4 quarts

Overnight Lasagna

1 lb. ground beef
½ cup onion, finely chopped
1 tsp. salt
1 (32 oz.) jar spaghetti sauce
1 cup water
2 tsp. oregano
Dash pepper
¼ tsp. sugar
1 egg, beaten
1 (15 oz.) container Ricotta cheese
½ cup Parmesan cheese, grated, divided
8 oz. Mozzarella cheese, shredded
1 tsp. parsley flakes
12 oz. lasagna noodles, uncooked

In a large skillet, brown ground beef. Add onion and salt; cook over medium heat 2–3 minutes, stirring frequently. Drain fat.

In a medium bowl, combine spaghetti sauce, water, oregano, pepper, and sugar.

In another bowl, combine egg, Ricotta cheese, ¼ cup Parmesan cheese, Mozzarella cheese, and parsley flakes.

Cover bottom of 9x13x2-inch baking dish with 1 cup spaghetti sauce mixture. Alternate layers of uncooked noodles, cheese mixture, ground beef, and spaghetti sauce, ending with sauce. Sprinkle remaining ¼ cup Parmesan cheese over top.

Cover and refrigerate overnight. Bake, covered with foil, at 350° for 45 minutes. Remove foil and bake an additional 15 minutes. Let stand 15 minutes before serving.

SERVES: 8–10

Marinara Sauce

6 slices bacon
3 onions, chopped
2 cloves garlic
2 (16 oz.) cans tomatoes
3 anchovies
3 whole cloves
1 tsp. dried oregano
3 sprigs parsley
  Salt and pepper to taste

Cut the bacon into ½-inch pieces. In a Dutch oven, fry until crisp. Remove bacon from drippings and set aside.

In the bacon drippings, sauté the onions and garlic until transparent. Add the tomatoes, anchovies, cloves, oregano, and parsley; salt and pepper.

Cook on low heat 1 hour. Let mixture cool slightly. Process in a blender or food processor until smooth. Add crisp bacon; reheat.

Serve immediately or refrigerate and reheat before serving.

SERVES: 8

Hearty Sausage Sauce

6 oz. lean bacon, diced

1 cup onion, chopped

6 cloves garlic, finely chopped

2½ lbs. mild Italian-style sausage, cut into ½-inch pieces

2 (28 oz.) cans chopped Italian-style tomatoes, undrained

2 (12 oz.) cans tomato juice

1 cup parsley, snipped

4 Tbsp. tomato paste

Salt and pepper to taste

2 small green peppers, seeded, cut into thin strips, optional

1 Tbsp. olive oil

Parmesan cheese, freshly grated

Mozzarella cheese

In a 3-quart saucepan, cook and stir the bacon over medium heat until golden, about 5 minutes. Stir in onion and garlic; cook until tender. Add in sausage pieces; cook until brown, about 5 minutes.

Stir tomatoes, tomato juice, and parsley into sausage mixture. Heat to boiling; reduce heat and cover. Simmer, stirring occasionally, for about 40 minutes. Uncover; stir in tomato paste. Cook over medium heat, stirring occasionally, until sauce is thickened, about 30 minutes. Season with salt and pepper as desired.

In a small skillet, cook and stir pepper strips in 1 tablespoon oil until barely tender, about 3 minutes. Stir into sauce. Sprinkle with Parmesan cheese.

NOTE: For an easy do ahead recipe, cook pasta and mix with a small amount of this sauce or any favorite pasta sauce. Put in a casserole large enough to hold pasta. Top with a generous amount of sauce and bake at 350° until bubbly. Generously cover top of sauce with Parmesan and Mozzarella cheese; broil until brown.

YIELD: 12 cups of sauce

Casablanca Rice

¼ cup butter

½ cup almonds, slivered and blanched

6 cups long-grain rice, cooked

2 (13¾ oz.) cans chicken broth

1 cup water

1 tsp. salt

½ tsp. ground cardamon

Dash pepper

2 Tbsp. orange peel, grated

1 cup white raisins

In a large saucepan, heat butter; sauté almonds until golden. Remove almonds and set aside.

In same saucepan with butter, combine rice, chicken broth, water, salt, cardamon, and pepper; mix well. Bring to a boil and cover. Simmer 5–7 minutes, until liquid is absorbed.

Add orange peel, raisins, and almonds. Toss with a fork until mixed well.

NOTE: Good with ham.

SERVES: 10–12

Chile Rice Casserole

6 cups cooked rice
½ lb. Monterey Jack
  or Cheddar cheese,
  shredded
1 (4 oz.) can
  green chiles
2 tsp. salt
1 tsp. pepper
2 cups sour cream
  Pimiento and/or
  parsley for garnish

In a large bowl, combine rice, cheese, chiles, and seasonings; fold in sour cream. Spoon mixture into a greased 8-cup mold or bundt pan; pack lightly with back of spoon.

Bake at 350° for 30 minutes. Unmold on serving platter and garnish with pimiento and/or parsley.

SERVES: 12

Sautéed Herbed Rice

4 Tbsp. butter
1 cup green onions,
  including tops,
  finely chopped
1 cup parsley, finely
  chopped
1 Tbsp. dillweed
2 cups rice, cooked
  and fluffed

In a large skillet, melt butter and sauté onion, parsley, and dill for 1 minute. Toss with hot rice. Serve immediately.

SERVES: 3–4

Green Rice

2 cups rice, cooked

2 eggs, beaten

1 cup milk

¼ cup oil

½ cup onion, chopped

½ tsp. garlic salt

Salt and pepper
to taste

1 (10 oz.) pkg.
frozen chopped
broccoli, thawed
and drained

1 lb. processed cheese
(Velveeta), cubed

 In a large bowl, combine all ingredients. Pour into greased 2-quart casserole dish.

Bake at 350° for 30–45 minutes or until center is firm.

SERVES: 6

Brown Rice Pilaf

½ cup golden raisins

½ cup Chablis or other dry white wine

¼ cup onion, chopped

¼ cup margarine, melted

1 cup brown rice, uncooked

1 tsp. salt

¼ tsp. pepper

2½ cups canned chicken broth

2 Tbsp. margarine, melted

½ cup cilantro, chopped

¾ cup slivered almonds, toasted

Fresh mint or cilantro sprigs, optional

 In a small bowl, combine raisins and wine; let stand 45 minutes. Drain and set aside.

In a large skillet, sauté onion in ¼ cup margarine until tender. Add rice; sauté 3 minutes. Add salt, pepper, and chicken broth. Bring to a boil; cover, reduce heat, and simmer 45 minutes or until rice is tender and liquid is absorbed.

Add raisins, 2 tablespoons margarine, cilantro, and almonds, stirring well.

Garnish with fresh mint sprigs, if desired.

SERVES: 4

Baked Wild Rice

4 (10½ oz.) cans
  beef broth
1½ cups wild rice
¼ cup butter
1 cup onion, chopped
1 cup mushrooms,
  chopped
1 cup half & half
  Salt and pepper
  to taste

In a 2-quart saucepan, heat beef broth to boiling. Add wild rice; cover and cook over low heat until most of the liquid is absorbed, 45–55 minutes.

In a large saucepan, melt butter. Add onions and mushrooms; sauté until onions are transparent. Add half & half; salt and pepper. Bring to a boil. Remove from heat.

Stir cooked wild rice into cream mixture. Transfer to a 2-quart greased casserole dish.

Cover and bake at 350° for 20 minutes.

SERVES: 4–6

Easy Browned Rice

1 cup rice, uncooked
¼ cup butter
1 (10½ oz.) can
  onion soup
1 (10½ oz.) can
  beef bouillon
¼ cup green pepper,
  finely diced

In a heavy skillet, brown raw rice on high heat until light brown. Remove from heat. Add butter and stir until melted. Add soups and green pepper. Turn into greased casserole dish.

Bake, covered, at 325° for 1 hour.

NOTE: A perfect accompaniment to go with Chicken in Sour Cream (see page 226).

SERVES: 4–6

Summer Rice Salad

3 cups steamed rice,
   cooled to room
   temperature

¼ cup mayonnaise

½ cup radishes,
   thinly sliced

½ cup scallions,
   thinly sliced

1 sweet red
   pepper, minced

1 green pepper,
   minced

2 Tbsp. sweet
   gherkins, minced

1 Tbsp. fresh
   parsley, minced

1 Tbsp. fresh dill,
   minced

1 Tbsp. fresh
   chives, snipped

½ cup fresh
   lemon juice

2 tsp. salt

2 garlic cloves,
   crushed

1¼ cups salad oil

Salt and freshly
   ground pepper
   to taste

 Combine first 10 ingredients and mix well; set aside.

Place lemon juice, salt, and garlic in a food processor or blender; mix well. With machine running, add oil in a thin stream until thoroughly incorporated. If added too fast, dressing may separate.

Add dressing to rice mixture; season with salt and pepper. Taste and adjust seasoning. Refrigerate.

Allow to return to room temperature before serving.

SERVES: 8–10

Saffron Couscous

1½ cups couscous
1½ cups chicken stock
⅛ tsp. saffron
2 Tbsp. butter
½ cup currants
½ bunch green
   onions, chopped
½ cup oil-cured black
   olives, pitted and
   slivered
Freshly ground
   pepper to taste

Put couscous in large bowl. In a saucepan, bring stock and saffron to a boil. Pour over couscous. Stir once or twice and cover bowl tightly with foil. Let steam for 10 minutes; fluff with fork. Add butter, currants, onions, olives, and pepper. Toss and serve immediately.

SERVES: 4

Couscous With Tomatoes

¼ lb. plum tomatoes
2 Tbsp. butter,
   divided
½ cup onion, finely
   chopped
¼ tsp. thread saffron
Salt and freshly
   ground pepper
   to taste
1⅓ cups water
1 cup couscous
3 Tbsp. fresh
   cilantro, finely
   chopped

Cut away cores of tomatoes. Cut tomatoes into ¼-inch cubes. There should be about ¾ cup.

In a saucepan, heat 1 tablespoon butter and add onion. Cook, stirring until transparent. Add saffron and stir. Add tomatoes and cook about 2 minutes, stirring. Add water; salt and pepper. Bring to boil.

Add couscous; stir and cover tightly. Remove from heat and let stand 5 minutes. Stir in cilantro and remaining tablespoon of butter and serve.

SERVES: 4

Couscous With Pine Nuts

½ lb. fresh mushrooms, sliced

¼ cup pine nuts

½ cup butter, melted and divided

1 cup onion, chopped

½ cup celery, chopped

½ cup fresh parsley, chopped

2 cloves garlic, minced

¼ cup dried currants

½ tsp. salt

½ tsp. pepper

½ tsp. herbes de Provence

3 cups canned chicken broth

1 (16 oz.) pkg. couscous

In a small skillet, sauté mushrooms and pine nuts in 2 tablespoons melted butter until mushrooms are tender. Remove from heat and set aside.

In a large skillet, sauté onion, celery, parsley, and garlic in remaining butter until tender. Add reserved mushroom mixture, currants, and seasonings; stir well. Add chicken broth; bring to a boil. Add couscous, stirring well.

Cover, remove from heat, and let stand 10 minutes or until liquid is absorbed.

SERVES: 16

Polenta

1½ cups cornmeal
1 tsp. salt
4½ cups water
6 Tbsp. butter
6 Tbsp. fresh
  Parmesan cheese,
  grated

In top of double boiler, mix cornmeal, salt, and 1½ cups cold water; stir until smooth. Stir in 3 cups boiling water. Cook over low heat for about an hour. (May be cooked over direct low heat for about 30 minutes if you have time to watch it and stir frequently.) Polenta is done when it pulls away from the sides while stirring.

Add butter and Parmesan cheese. Serve hot.

NOTE: With leftovers, spread on a flat pan about ¼-inch thick, and store for the next meal. Cut in circles with a biscuit cutter. Place overlapping in a pan; sprinkle with Parmesan cheese or favorite meat sauce. Bake at 350° until warm.

YIELD: 5 cups

Hearty Cheese Grits

6 cups water
½ tsp. salt
1½ cups regular grits, uncooked
½ cup margarine
4 cups medium sharp Cheddar cheese, shredded and divided
3 eggs, beaten

In a large pan, combine water and salt; bring to a boil. Stir in grits; cook until done. Remove from heat; add margarine and 3¾ cups of cheese. Stir grits until cheese melts.

Add a small amount of grits to eggs; add to remaining grits. Pour mixture into lightly greased 2½-quart baking dish.

Bake at 350° for 1 hour and 10 minutes. Sprinkle with remaining cheese and bake an additional 5 minutes.

SERVES: 8

Barley Casserole

½ cup margarine
1 cup onion, diced
1 cup barley
1 (4 oz.) can sliced mushrooms, drained
2 (10 oz.) cans chicken broth plus 1 can water
½ cup sliced almonds
1 cup peas, optional
Salt and pepper to taste

Melt margarine in a large skillet. Sauté onion until tender. Add barley and mushrooms; cook, stirring 5–7 minutes. Add broth and water; bring to a boil. Add almonds, salt and pepper; peas, if desired. Place in an 8x12-inch ungreased baking dish. Bake at 300° for 1 hour.

NOTE: Great with chicken, pork, or Cornish hens.

SERVES: 6–8

Baked Hungarian Noodles

1 lb. fine egg noodles, cooked

4 cups sour cream

4 cups cottage cheese

1 cup onion, finely minced

4 cloves garlic, minced

4 Tbsp. Worcestershire sauce

4 dashes Tabasco

4 Tbsp. poppy seeds

6 Tbsp. Parmesan cheese, divided

Salt and pepper to taste

Paprika

 Cook noodles according to package directions; drain well.

In a 3-quart casserole dish, combine hot noodles with sour cream, cottage cheese, onion, garlic, Worcestershire sauce, Tabasco, poppy seeds, and 4 tablespoons of Parmesan cheese; salt and pepper. Top with paprika and remaining Parmesan cheese.

Bake at 350° for 30 minutes or until bubbly.

SERVES: 12

1919, Age 34

A Bess Recipe

Mrs. Truman's Cheese Soufflé

4 tablespoons butter
2 tablespoons flour
1 cup scalded milk or tomato juice
$\frac{1}{2}$ cup grated cheese
4 egg yolks (beaten light)
4 egg whites (beaten stiff)
Few grains cayenne
$\frac{1}{2}$ teaspoon salt

Melt butter, add flour. Gradually add the scalded milk or tomato juice, and stir until thick and smooth. Add salt, cayenne and cheese. Stir until smooth. Remove from fire, add yolks. Cool, cut and fold in whites.

Pour into buttered baking dish or ramekins. Set in pan of hot water. If desired firm, bake 30 to 45 minutes in a moderately slow oven (325°). If desired soft, bake 20 minutes in moderately hot oven (375°). Serve at once.

Serves four.

ABOVE: Harry, Bess and Margaret Truman pose in front of an automobile, August, 1934.

BELOW: The Trumans enjoy the climate of Key West, Florida, in November, 1951.

Saucy Spring Asparagus

2 lbs. fresh asparagus
¼ cup butter
½ tsp. salt
⅛ tsp. pepper
½ tsp. dried thyme

 Wash asparagus. Snap off ends. Cut diagonally into 2-inch pieces.

Melt butter in large skillet. Add asparagus and sprinkle with seasonings.

Cover and cook over medium-high heat about 5 minutes, stirring occasionally until stalk is just crisp-tender.

Serve with Vegetable Sauce.

SERVES: 4–6

Vegetable Sauce

¼ cup margarine,
*   melted*
1 cup mayonnaise
2 Tbsp. horseradish
2 Tbsp. onion, grated
¼ tsp. cayenne pepper
½ tsp. Tabasco sauce
1 tsp. dry mustard

 In a small mixing bowl, combine all ingredients, blending well; refrigerate.

To serve, heat and pour over the steamed vegetable of your choice.

NOTE: This is best if made 1 day ahead.

YIELD: 1½ cups

Hawaiian Baked Beans

¾ cup catsup

¾ cup brown sugar

1 Tbsp. Worcestershire sauce

½ cup onion, chopped

1 lb. ground beef

1 lb. bacon, cooked and crumbled

1 (10 oz.) pkg. Polish sausage, cooked and sliced

2 (16 oz.) cans baked beans, drained

1 (16 oz.) can butter beans, drained

1 (16 oz.) can kidney beans, drained

1 (16 oz.) can lima beans, drained

1 (16 oz.) can pineapple chunks, drained

1 cup processed cheese (Velveeta), cubed

In a small bowl, make sauce by combining catsup, brown sugar, Worcestershire sauce, and onion; set aside.

In a skillet, brown ground beef; drain. Cook bacon until done, but not too crispy. Cook Polish sausage and cut into ¼-inch slices.

Place all beans, pineapple, meats, and cheese in a large baking pan and pour sauce over top; mix well.

Bake at 350° for 45 minutes.

SERVES: 16

Four Bean Casserole

8 slices bacon, cut
   in ½-inch pieces
4 large onions, cut
   in rings
¾ cup brown sugar
1 tsp. dry mustard
1 tsp. garlic powder
1 tsp. salt
½ cup cider vinegar
1 (15 oz.) can large
   butter beans,
   drained
1 (16 oz.) can cut
   green beans,
   drained
1 (16 oz.) can red
   kidney beans,
   undrained
1 (11 oz.) jar Boston
   baked beans

In a skillet, brown bacon and remove to drain. Cook onions in bacon drippings until transparent. Add sugar, seasonings, and vinegar; cook 20 minutes.

Combine beans, reserved bacon, and onion mixture in a 3-quart greased casserole.

Bake uncovered at 350° for 1 hour.

SERVES: 10–12

Red Beans and Rice

1½ lbs. ground beef

3 garlic cloves, minced

1 cup onion, chopped

3 (16 oz.) cans kidney beans, undrained

2 (16 oz.) cans Italian-style tomatoes

1 (16 oz.) can Cajun-style tomatoes

1 (4 oz.) can sliced mushrooms

1½ tsp. salt

1 tsp. pepper

½ tsp. Tabasco sauce

¼ cup soy sauce

2 Tbsp. Worcestershire sauce

½ tsp. onion powder

½ tsp. garlic salt

1 (12 oz.) pkg. Polish sausage, optional

4 cups white rice, cooked

In a large skillet, brown beef, garlic, and onions; drain. Add beans, tomatoes, mushrooms, and spices to ground beef; simmer for 30 minutes.

Cut Polish sausage into bite-size pieces; brown in skillet or broil in oven until lightly crisp. Add to beans and simmer 10 minutes longer.

Cook rice according to package directions.

Serve mixture over hot rice.

SERVES: 6–8

Camelot Beans

6 slices bacon

1 cup onion, chopped

2 medium apples, peeled, cored, and chopped

2 medium green peppers, seeded and chopped

3 tsp. curry powder

4 (16 oz.) cans red kidney beans, drained and rinsed

2 (16 oz.) cans whole tomatoes, half the liquid reserved

2 cups dark brown sugar

Parmesan cheese, grated

In a medium skillet, cook bacon; drain and crumble, reserving drippings. Sauté onions, apples, and peppers in drippings until soft.

To onion mixture, add crumbled bacon, curry, beans, tomatoes with reserved liquid, and sugar; mix well.

Place in a 3-quart casserole and top with cheese.

Bake at 350° for 1 hour.

NOTE: May be frozen.

SERVES: 16–20

Barbecued Beans

8 oz. sliced bacon,
  chopped

1½ cups onion,
  chopped

1 large green pepper,
  chopped

1 large red bell
  pepper, chopped

1 cup dark brown
  sugar, packed

1 cup tomato-based
  barbecue sauce
  (hot, sweet, or
  hickory-flavored)

⅔ cup maple-flavored
  pancake syrup

⅓ cup light corn
  syrup

3 (28 oz.) cans pork
  and beans, drained

⅔ cup beer or
  apple juice

1 lb. ground beef,
  optional

Pulverized burned
  ends of grilled
  briskets, optional

In a heavy skillet, fry bacon over medium heat until lightly browned. Add onion and peppers; cook 3 minutes or until vegetables are crisp-tender. Stir in sugar, barbecue sauce, and syrups.

Pour beans into a 9x13-inch pan. Add bacon mixture and beer; stir to mix. Brisket or browned meat may be added at this point, if desired.

Grill over hickory chips for optimum smoky flavor or bake in oven at 325° for 2–3 hours.

SERVES: 8–12

Sweet and Sour Green Beans

6 slices bacon
½ cup onion, chopped
3 Tbsp. sugar
1 Tbsp. vinegar
1 (16 oz.) can French-style green beans, drained
3 Tbsp. slivered almonds

 Cook bacon until crisp; drain and crumble, reserving 3 tablespoons bacon drippings.

Sauté onion in reserved bacon drippings until transparent. Mix in the sugar and vinegar.

Place green beans in 1½-quart greased baking dish. Pour onion mixture on top and marinate overnight in refrigerator.

When ready to bake, top with reserved bacon and almonds.

Bake at 350° for 30 minutes.

SERVES: 4

Green Bean Packages

2 (16 oz.) cans whole green beans, drained
Red pepper, cut into ¼-inch strips, optional
½ lb. bacon
Garlic salt or Creole seasoning to taste
Salt and pepper to taste

Wrap 4–5 beans and 2–3 red pepper strips in ½-slice bacon. Secure with wooden pick and place in oven-proof greased dish.

Season with garlic salt; salt and pepper.

Broil in oven until bacon is done, about 5–8 minutes.

NOTE: For variation: after broiling, place beans in heated mixture of liquid from 1 can green beans combined with 1 cup brown sugar.

SERVES: 6–8

Herbed Broccoli

2 chicken bouillon
   cubes
1 cup water
¼ cup onion, chopped
1 tsp. dried
   marjoram
1 tsp. dried basil
1½ lbs. fresh broccoli
3 Tbsp. butter, melted

In a large skillet, combine bouillon cubes and water; cook over medium heat until bouillon dissolves. Stir in onion and herbs.

Add broccoli to liquid; cover and reduce heat. Simmer 10 minutes or until tender.

Drain and arrange broccoli on a serving platter; drizzle with melted butter.

SERVES: 6

Broccoli Corn Bake

1 (10 oz.) pkg.
   frozen chopped
   broccoli, cooked
   and drained
1 (16 oz.) can
   cream-style corn
1 egg, beaten
1 cup saltine
   crackers, crushed,
   divided
2 Tbsp. onion,
   minced
3 Tbsp. butter,
   melted, divided
½ tsp. salt
⅛ tsp. pepper

In a large mixing bowl, mix broccoli, corn, beaten egg, ½ cup cracker crumbs, onion, 2 tablespoons butter, salt, and pepper. Pour into a greased 1-quart casserole dish.

Bake at 350° for 35–40 minutes.

Combine remaining cracker crumbs and 1 tablespoon butter. Sprinkle over vegetable mixture the last 15 minutes of baking time.

SERVES: 6

Broccoli With Browned Butter

4½ lbs. fresh broccoli
1 cup butter
12 lemon slices

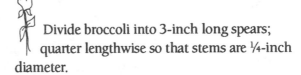 Divide broccoli into 3-inch long spears; quarter lengthwise so that stems are ¼-inch diameter.

Fifteen minutes before serving, melt butter in a saucepan over medium heat. To clarify butter, skim off foam as it appears and continue cooking butter until lightly browned. Set aside and keep warm.

In an open stock pot, cook broccoli in boiling, salted water for 4 minutes. Cover and cook an additional 1–2 minutes or until broccoli is bright green; drain.

Arrange broccoli on warm serving dish and spoon browned butter over broccoli. Garnish with lemon slices. Serve immediately.

SERVES: 12

Creamy Broccoli Casserole

4 cups fresh broccoli, cut into 1-inch pieces

½ (10¾ oz.) can cream of mushroom soup

1 (3 oz.) jar pimientos

1 cup sour cream

1 cup celery, sliced

1 Tbsp. Worcestershire sauce

1 Tbsp. dry onion flakes

Salt and pepper to taste

½ cup Cheddar cheese, grated

In a large bowl, combine all ingredients except cheese; mix well. Pour into greased 3-quart baking dish. Top with grated cheese.

Bake at 350° for 1 hour.

SERVES: 6 – 8

Carrot Bake

½ cup onion, chopped

4 Tbsp. margarine

2 lbs. carrots, sliced
½-inch thick

½ lb. processed cheese
(Velveeta), cubed

½ cup buttery
crackers, crushed

 In a small skillet, simmer the onions in the margarine until transparent; set aside.

In a small saucepan, cook carrots in water to cover until tender; drain.

In a 1½-quart baking dish, layer the carrots and cubed cheese. Pour the onions over the carrots and top with crushed crackers.

Bake at 350° for 30 minutes.

NOTE: For a crunchy flavor, add water chestnuts. Crushed potato chips may be used instead of crackers.

SERVES: 6

Cranberry Carrots

3 lbs. carrots,
diagonally cut

½ cup butter

¾ cup jellied
cranberry sauce

½ cup brown sugar,
firmly packed

¾ tsp. salt

 In a large saucepan, cover carrots with water and cook for 8–10 minutes; drain.

In a separate saucepan, melt butter and add cranberry sauce, brown sugar, and salt. Cook and stir constantly until smooth.

Pour over carrots and toss to coat.

NOTE: Pressing the cranberry sauce through a sieve before heating helps to eliminate lumps.

SERVES: 10

Layered Carrot and Parsnip Polenta

1 lb. carrots, cut into chunks

1 lb. parsnips, cut into chunks

6 Tbsp. butter, divided

1 cup whipping cream

Salt and pepper to taste

⅛ tsp. nutmeg, freshly grated

1 cup yellow cornmeal, finely ground

4 cups chicken stock, divided

3 eggs, room temperature, separated

3 Tbsp. dry bread crumbs

¼ cup parsley, chopped

In a saucepan, cook carrots in salted boiling water until soft; drain well. Cook parsnips in another pan and drain well.

Transfer carrots to food processor; add 2 tablespoons butter and process. Gradually add some of the cream until purée is spreadable, about ⅓ to ½ cup. Pour into bowl and season with salt and pepper; set aside.

Repeat above process with parsnips, season with nutmeg; salt and pepper. Set aside.

In a medium bowl, combine cornmeal and 1 cup cold chicken stock; mix well.

In a medium saucepan, heat remaining 3 cups chicken stock to boiling. Whisk the cornmeal mixture (polenta) into boiling stock. Cook over medium-high heat until mixture thickens, stirring constantly with wooden spoon, about 15 minutes. Remove from heat; cool 15 minutes.

In a small bowl, whisk egg yolks; add ½ cup polenta mixture and stir. Blend yolk mixture back into polenta in saucepan.

In a large bowl, beat egg whites with a pinch of salt until stiff. Stir ¼ of egg whites into polenta to lighten; fold in remaining beaten eggs.

Layered Polenta,
continued

Butter a 3-quart baking dish. Sprinkle bottom with bread crumbs.

Layer ⅓ polenta in prepared dish; top with carrot purée. Layer another ⅓ polenta; top with parsnip puree and sprinkle with parsley. Top with remaining polenta. Dot with remaining 2 tablespoons butter.

Bake at 350° for 45–55 minutes or until slightly puffed and browned.

NOTE: Consider substitutes such as sweet potatoes and broccoli for another interesting blend of flavors.

SERVES: 8

Boston Baked Corn

2 tsp. dry mustard
1 tsp. salt
¼ cup brown sugar
1¼ cups catsup
1 cup onion, diced
2 (15 oz.) cans
    whole kernel corn,
    drained
6 slices bacon, diced

 Combine first four ingredients in medium bowl. Add onion and corn; mix thoroughly.

Pour into greased 1½-quart casserole; top with bacon.

Bake at 350° for 40 minutes, or until bacon is cooked.

SERVES: 6–8

Jacomo Corn Bake

1 (16 oz.) pkg. frozen whole kernel corn

¾ cup Swiss cheese, shredded

¾ cup Monterey Jack cheese, shredded

2 eggs, beaten

¾ cup evaporated milk

1 (10¾ oz.) can cream of mushroom soup

1 (4 oz.) jar sliced mushrooms, drained

1 (2 oz.) jar pimientos, drained

¼ cup onion, finely chopped

⅓ cup green pepper, finely chopped

1 (2½ oz.) can French-fried onion rings

Salt and pepper to taste

¾ cup soft wheat bread crumbs

2 Tbsp. butter, melted

 Cook frozen corn according to package directions; drain.

In a separate bowl, mix cheeses together; set aside. In a medium bowl, combine 1 cup of the cheese mixture, eggs, milk, soup, mushrooms, pimientos, onion, green pepper, and ½ can of the French-fried onion rings; salt and pepper. Stir in corn.

Pour mixture into a 1½ -quart buttered casserole or quiche dish. Place dish on baking sheet.

Bake at 350° for 40 minutes.

Toss bread crumbs with butter; add remaining cheese and French-fried onion rings. Spread on top of casserole.

Bake 5–10 minutes longer or until golden brown.

SERVES: 8

Lebanese Eggplant Casserole

1 medium eggplant, peeled

¼ cup slivered almonds

¼ cup olive oil

½ cup onion, chopped

2 garlic cloves, crushed

½ cup mushrooms, sliced

2 Tbsp. flour

1 (16 oz.) can tomatoes

½ tsp. brown sugar

½ tsp. salt

⅛ tsp. pepper

¼ tsp. dried basil

1 Tbsp. Parmesan cheese, grated

 Cut eggplant into ½-inch rounds. Parboil in salted water for 10 minutes; drain well.

In a skillet, sauté slivered almonds in olive oil for 5 minutes. Remove almonds; set aside.

In the same skillet, sauté onion, garlic, and mushrooms until onion is golden; add flour and mix well. Add tomatoes, brown sugar, salt, pepper, and basil. Cook over medium heat, stirring mixture until it comes to a boil and thickens slightly.

In lightly greased 1-quart casserole dish, alternate layers of eggplant with tomato mixture. Sprinkle with Parmesan cheese and almonds.

Bake at 375° for 25 minutes.

SERVES: 6

Stuffed Vidalia Onions

4 medium Vidalia
  onions
2 Tbsp. oil-free
  Italian dressing
½ cup sweet red
  pepper, chopped
1 cup zucchini,
  chopped
½ cup soft bread
  crumbs
½ cup part-skim
  Mozzarella cheese,
  shredded
2 Tbsp. fresh parsley,
  minced
¼ tsp. dried oregano
  Dash Tabasco
  Paprika, optional
  Fresh parsley
  sprigs, optional

 Peel onions. Cut a slice from the top and the bottom; chop slices and set aside.

In a large skillet, steam onions in a small amount of boiling water for 15–20 minutes or until tender. Cool. Remove center of onions, leaving shells intact. Reserve centers for use in other recipes. Set onion shells aside.

Heat Italian dressing in medium skillet until hot. Add reserved chopped onion, red pepper, and zucchini; sauté until tender. Remove from heat; stir in bread crumbs, cheese, minced parsley, oregano, and Tabasco.

Fill each shell with ½ cup vegetable mixture. Place in an 8-inch square baking dish coated with cooking spray.

Cover and bake at 350° for 20 minutes. Uncover and bake additional 5 minutes. Garnish with paprika and parsley sprigs.

SERVES: 4

Make Ahead Mashed Potatoes

5 lbs. potatoes,
  peeled and
  quartered
1 (8 oz.) pkg.
  cream cheese
1 cup sour cream
2 tsp. onion salt
1 tsp. salt
1/4 tsp. pepper
2 Tbsp. butter
1/2 cup milk, optional
  Cheese, grated
  for topping

Using large heavy saucepan, cook potatoes in boiling water until tender; drain well. Return potatoes to pan and mash until smooth. Add cream cheese, sour cream, and seasonings; beat until fluffy. If potatoes seem dry, add up to 1/2 cup milk.

Place potato mixture in airtight container and store in refrigerator.

When ready to serve, place desired amount of potatoes in greased casserole dish. Bake at 350° for 30 minutes or until heated thoroughly.

Dot casserole with butter the last 10 minutes. Top with grated cheese.

NOTE: This recipe will keep for 2 weeks in the refrigerator.

SERVES: 12

Garlic Mashed Potatoes

3 lbs. medium-size
   red-skinned
   potatoes
6 large cloves
   garlic, unpeeled
½ cup extra virgin
   olive oil, plus
   additional, for
   drizzle if desired
Salt and freshly
   ground pepper
   to taste

Place unpeeled potatoes and garlic in a
pot and cover with water. Bring to a boil
over high heat; reduce to a simmer and cook
uncovered until the potatoes are tender,
35–45 minutes.

Drain the potatoes and garlic. Return the
potatoes to pot, reserving the garlic; cook over
medium heat for 1–2 minutes to evaporate any
excess liquid.

Place the potatoes in a large mixing bowl.
Squeeze the garlic pulp from the skins and add
to the potatoes. Beat the potatoes with a hand-
held electric mixer until fluffy.

With the mixer running, slowly beat in the olive
oil. Season the potatoes with salt and pepper;
serve at once. It is nice to drizzle each serving
with a little additional olive oil.

SERVES: 6–8

Party Potatoes

4 (16 oz.) cans
whole potatoes,
sliced

1 cup mayonnaise

1 lb. sharp cheese,
grated

¾ cup onion, chopped

3 Tbsp. parsley,
chopped

Salt and pepper
to taste

¼ cup stuffed green
olives, halved

4 strips bacon,
uncooked

In a large mixing bowl, combine potatoes, mayonnaise, cheese, onion, and parsley; salt and pepper. Place in a greased 2-quart casserole dish.

Bake, covered, at 350° for 45 minutes. During final 25 minutes, uncover and top with green olives and bacon strips.

SERVES: 12

Potatoes Parmesan

6 medium potatoes,
unpeeled and cut
into chunks

1 medium onion,
cut into chunks

¼ cup butter

1 clove garlic,
minced

½ tsp. salt

¼ tsp. pepper

½ tsp. celery seed

½ cup Parmesan
cheese, grated

Place the unpeeled potatoes in the bottom of a 9x13-inch pan; layer the onion chunks between the potatoes.

In a small saucepan, melt butter; add garlic and drizzle over the potatoes. Sprinkle with salt, pepper, and celery seed.

Cover with foil and bake at 400° for 45 minutes. Remove the foil and sprinkle with cheese. Bake uncovered 20 minutes longer, or until tender.

SERVES: 6

Surely the Best Potatoes

2½ lbs. potatoes,
   peeled and cooked
3 cups cottage cheese
¾ cup sour cream
1½ Tbsp. onion, grated
1½ tsp. salt
¼ cup butter, melted
½ cup sliced almonds,
   toasted

 For the best results, this recipe should be made 1 day ahead.

Mash the potatoes until smooth, and combine with the cottage cheese, sour cream, onion, and salt.

Place in a 2-quart round or 9x13-inch baking dish.

Bake at 350° for 30 minutes, uncovered. Remove from oven and cool; refrigerate until the next day.

When ready to serve, bake at 350° for 25 minutes. Top with melted butter and place under broiler until brown. Sprinkle toasted almonds on top.

NOTE: This recipe also works well with a favorite gravy, although you may want to omit the butter and almonds.

SERVES: 8–10

Celeried Potato Puffs

1 cup celery, minced

3 Tbsp. butter, melted, divided

¼ cup shallots, minced

2 lbs. potatoes, peeled and quartered

½ cup half & half

¼ tsp. salt

⅛ tsp. pepper

3 egg yolks, beaten

½ cup Parmesan cheese, grated

Celery leaves, optional

In a small skillet, sauté celery in 2 tablespoons butter until crisp-tender; add shallots and sauté 2 minutes. Set aside.

In a medium pan, cook potatoes in boiling, salted water 15 minutes or until tender; drain and mash.

In a saucepan, combine half & half and 1 tablespoon butter. Heat until butter melts, stirring occasionally. Stir into mashed potatoes; add salt and pepper.

Add ½ cup potatoes to egg yolks; mix well. Combine with remaining potatoes. Stir in celery mixture and Parmesan cheese.

Spoon potato mixture into 5 lightly greased 6-ounce custard cups. Set custard cups in a 9x13-inch pan; pour hot water into pan to a depth of 1 inch, surrounding custard cups.

Bake at 450° for 30 minutes or until knife inserted in center comes out clean.

Unmold onto a serving platter or individual dish. Garnish with celery leaves, if desired.

SERVES: 6

Special Spuds

3 lbs. white potatoes, scrubbed

½ cup butter, melted

2½ cups Cheddar cheese, shredded and divided

½ cup green onions, chopped

2 cups sour cream

2 tsp. salt

¼ tsp. pepper

Paprika to taste

 Bake potatoes at 400° for 40 minutes or until slightly firm. Cool overnight.

The next day, peel and grate potatoes. In a large bowl, combine potatoes with butter, 2 cups cheese, onions, sour cream, salt, and pepper.

Pour into a greased 3-quart casserole dish.

Bake at 350° for 30–40 minutes. During final 15 minutes, top with remaining cheese and paprika.

SERVES: 14–16

Potatoes Amandine

2 baking potatoes
4 Tbsp. butter
½ cup boiling water
¾ cup flour, divided
2 eggs
½ tsp. salt
⅛ tsp. pepper
¼ tsp. nutmeg
1 egg, beaten
1 cup sliced almonds, chopped
Oil for deep frying

 Bake potatoes in 425° oven for 1 hour, until tender.

In a small saucepan, melt butter in ½ cup boiling water. Add ½ cup flour all at once; stir vigorously. Cook and stir until mixture forms a ball that doesn't separate. Remove from heat; cool slightly. Add 2 eggs, one at a time, beating after each until smooth.

Peel the hot potatoes; mash. Season with salt and pepper; add nutmeg. Add potatoes to cooked flour mixture; mix well. Chill.

Using 1 rounded tablespoon dough, form into sixteen 2-inch logs. Dip in additional ¼ cup flour, then in beaten egg. Roll in almonds.

Heat ½-inch oil in 10-inch skillet. Fry half the rolls at a time, about 2 minutes, turning once.

SERVES: 8

Rutabagas With Garlic and Greens

2 Tbsp. olive oil

¾ lb. rutabagas, peeled and cut into ¾-inch pieces

4 medium cloves garlic, finely chopped

½ cup Swiss chard or spinach leaves, finely chopped

1 cup onion, chopped

1¼ cups chicken, beef or vegetable broth

Salt and freshly ground pepper to taste

Few drops lemon juice, optional

In a deep skillet, heat 1 tablespoon of oil over medium heat; add rutabagas and sauté for 3 minutes. Remove rutabagas with slotted spoon; set aside.

In the liquid that remains, add garlic and sauté for 15 seconds. Add chard and sauté 30 seconds longer, stirring continuously. Remove and set aside.

Heat the remaining tablespoon of oil. Add onion and sauté over medium heat until brown. Add broth and bring to boil.

Add rutabagas; reduce heat. Cover and simmer for 25 minutes.

Add chard mixture and cook until rutabagas are tender, about 10 minutes, adding a few tablespoons of water if pan becomes dry. Season with salt and pepper. Add lemon juice, if desired. Serve hot.

SERVES: 2–3

Rutabagas With Raisins

1 Tbsp. oil

1 large onion, sliced

1½ lbs. rutabagas, peeled and cut into 1-inch pieces

1 tsp. paprika

1¼ cups water

Salt and freshly ground pepper to taste

¼ cup dark raisins

Cayenne pepper to taste

Heat the oil in a large saucepan. Add onion and sauté over medium heat until transparent.

Add rutabagas, paprika, and water; salt and pepper. Bring to a boil. Reduce heat to a simmer; cover. Cook until tender, about 45 minutes, adding a few tablespoons water if mixture becomes dry during cooking.

Add the raisins. If too much liquid remains, uncover pan and cook 5 minutes longer. Add cayenne; adjust for seasonings.

SERVES: 3–4

Yellow Squash Casserole

2 lbs. yellow or zucchini squash, sliced ¼-inch thick

1 cup water

1 cup onion, finely chopped

2 Tbsp. butter, melted

1 cup buttery crackers, crushed and divided

1½ cups Cheddar cheese, shredded

2 eggs, beaten

¼ tsp. salt

¼ tsp. pepper

In a medium saucepan, bring 1 cup water to a boil; add squash and simmer for 10 minutes. Drain and set aside.

In a large skillet, sauté onion in butter until tender.

Combine squash with onions; add ¾ cup cracker crumbs, cheese, eggs, salt, and pepper. Mix well.

Pour mixture into lightly greased 2-quart casserole. Sprinkle with remaining crumbs.

Bake uncovered at 350° for 45 minutes.

NOTE: Doubling this recipe will fill a 9x13-inch baking dish.

SERVES: 6

Squash Soufflé

4 small yellow or
  zucchini squash,
  sliced into ½-inch
  rounds
1 (3 oz.) pkg.
  cream cheese
3 eggs, beaten
1 tsp. garlic salt
½ cup onion, chopped
½ cup Parmesan
  cheese, grated
  Paprika to taste

In a medium saucepan, cover squash with water and cook until tender; drain. Mash and add cream cheese, eggs, garlic salt, and onion.

Pour into 1½-quart baking dish. Top with Parmesan cheese and sprinkle with paprika.

Bake at 325° for 30–45 minutes.

SERVES: 6

Spaghetti Squash Casserole

1 (8-inch) spaghetti squash

2 Tbsp. butter or olive oil

1 cup onion, chopped

½ lb. fresh mushrooms, sliced

2 medium garlic cloves, crushed

¼ cup fresh parsley, finely chopped

1 tsp. basil

½ tsp. oregano

Dash of thyme

Salt and pepper to taste

2 medium tomatoes, chopped

1 cup Ricotta cheese

1 cup Mozzarella cheese, grated

1 cup fine bread crumbs

Parmesan cheese, grated for garnish

Slice squash in half lengthwise and scoop out seeds. Place face down in a buttered pan and bake at 350° for 30 minutes. Cool and scoop out the pulp; reserve.

In a medium skillet, heat butter or olive oil; sauté onion, mushrooms, garlic, and herbs; salt and pepper. When onions are tender, add fresh tomatoes. Cook until most of the liquid evaporates.

Combine squash, tomato mixture, cheeses, and bread crumbs. Pour into a buttered 2-quart casserole dish. Top with Parmesan.

Bake at 375° for 35–40 minutes, uncovered.

SERVES: 6–8

Butternut Squash Risotto

1 medium butternut
  squash
6 cups chicken stock,
  divided
2 Tbsp. unsalted
  butter, divided
1 Tbsp. olive oil
4 shallots, peeled
  and minced
2 cups Arborio rice
½ cup dry white wine
  Freshly grated
  nutmeg
  Salt and freshly
  ground pepper
  to taste
1 Tbsp. fresh
  rosemary, chopped
½ cup Parmesan
  cheese, grated,
  divided
  Rosemary sprigs
  for garnish

Cut squash into eighths; discard seeds. Steam squash for 10–11 minutes or until tender. Scoop flesh from skin and mash lightly.

In a 2-quart saucepan, heat stock to a simmer and set aside.

In a large, heavy saucepan over medium heat, melt 1 tablespoon butter. Add oil and shallots; cook for 2 minutes. Add rice; cook, stirring for 5 minutes.

Add wine to rice; cook, stirring, until wine is nearly absorbed. Stir in squash and 1 cup stock; cook at a steady simmer until liquid is nearly absorbed. Stir in remaining stock, 1 cup at a time, until rice is creamy and firm, but not hard in the center, 15–20 minutes.

Add chopped rosemary and nutmeg; salt and pepper. Stir in remaining butter and most of the Parmesan, reserving some for garnish.

Serve in shallow bowls garnished with cheese and rosemary sprigs.

SERVES: 4–6

Autumn Butternut Casserole

3 cups butternut
squash, chopped
in large pieces

6 Tbsp. butter

1 Tbsp. brown sugar

¼ tsp. salt

⅛ tsp. white pepper

2 lbs. Jonathan
apples, unpeeled
and sliced

¼ cup sugar

1½ cups corn flakes,
coarsely crushed

½ cup pecans,
chopped

½ cup brown sugar

2 Tbsp. butter, melted

In a large saucepan, cook squash in boiling water until tender; drain well. Mash squash; season with 4 tablespoons butter, brown sugar, salt, and pepper.

Heat 2 tablespoons of butter in a skillet; add sliced apples and sprinkle with ¼ cup sugar. Cover and simmer over low heat until barely tender, about 5 minutes.

Place cooked apples in a 3-quart casserole dish and cover evenly with squash.

Mix corn flakes with pecans, brown sugar, and melted butter. Sprinkle over squash.

Bake at 350° for 15 minutes.

SERVES: 8

Spinach Supreme

2 (10 oz.) pkgs.
frozen chopped
spinach

2 Tbsp. onion,
chopped

4 Tbsp. butter, melted

2 Tbsp. flour

½ cup evaporated
milk

½ tsp. pepper

¾ tsp. garlic salt

¾ tsp. salt

1 tsp. Worcestershire
sauce

1 (6 oz.) roll
jalapeño cheese,
cubed

Buttered bread
crumbs

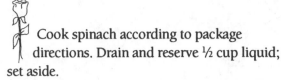 Cook spinach according to package directions. Drain and reserve ½ cup liquid; set aside.

In a small skillet, sauté onion in butter until tender. Add flour, stirring until blended and smooth. Slowly add reserved liquid and milk, stirring constantly. Cook until thickened.

Add pepper, garlic salt, salt, Worcestershire sauce, and cheese; stir until cheese is melted.

Combine sauce and spinach. Pour into a greased 2-quart casserole dish; top with buttered bread crumbs.

Bake at 350° until bubbly.

SERVES: 8

Cheesy Spinach Casserole

2 (10 oz.) pkgs. frozen chopped spinach

½ cup cracker crumbs

2 Tbsp. margarine, melted

1 pkg. dry onion soup mix

2 cups sour cream

1½ cups Cheddar cheese, grated, divided

 Cook spinach according to directions. Drain well; set aside.

Mix cracker crumbs with margarine; set aside.

In a large mixing bowl, combine soup mix, sour cream, 1 cup cheese and spinach.

Pour mixture into greased 9x12-inch baking dish; top with remaining cheese. Sprinkle reserved crumbs over cheese.

Bake at 300° for 45 minutes. Cover top of casserole with aluminum foil if crumbs get too dark.

SERVES: 6–8

Tomato Rockefeller

18 tomato slices, approximately 2-inches thick

2 (10 oz.) pkgs. frozen chopped spinach

1 cup soft bread crumbs

1 cup green onions, chopped

6 eggs, beaten

¾ cup butter, melted

½ cup Parmesan cheese, grated

½ tsp. garlic, minced

1 tsp. salt

1 tsp. thyme

Tabasco to taste

 Arrange tomatoes on a lightly greased jelly roll pan.

Cook spinach according to package directions; drain.

In a large bowl, combine spinach, bread crumbs, onions, eggs, butter, Parmesan cheese, garlic, salt, thyme, and Tabasco; mix well.

Mound equal amounts of mixture on tomatoes.

Bake at 350° for 15 minutes or until set.

SERVES: 18

Thumbs-Up Turnips

4 cups turnips,
  peeled and sliced

⅓ cup onion, chopped

2 tsp. sugar

2 eggs, beaten

1 tsp. garlic salt

½ tsp. pepper

1 (10¾ oz.) can
  cream of
  mushroom soup

½ cup cracker
  crumbs

1 Tbsp. Parmesan
  cheese, grated

4 Tbsp. margarine,
  melted

Place turnips, onion, and sugar in a large saucepan; add water to cover. Bring to a boil over high heat. Reduce heat and simmer until turnips are tender but not soft; drain.

In a large bowl, combine the turnip mixture, eggs, garlic salt, pepper, and soup; mix well. Spoon into a buttered 2-quart casserole.

In a small bowl, mix cracker crumbs and cheese; sprinkle over turnip mixture. Drizzle with margarine.

Bake at 350° for 30 minutes, or until top is golden brown.

SERVES: 6

Zucchini Extra

2 Tbsp. butter
½ cup onion, chopped
1 clove garlic, chopped
4 zucchini, sliced in ½-inch pieces
2 tomatoes, coarsely chopped
1 tsp. salt
⅛ tsp. pepper
¼ tsp. oregano

 In a large skillet, sauté melted butter, onion, and garlic until tender. Add zucchini and tomatoes. Season with salt, pepper, and oregano.

Cover and cook 10–15 minutes or until zucchini is tender.

SERVES: 4–6

Zucchini With Pecans

2 Tbsp. pecans, chopped
Vegetable cooking spray
1½ cups zucchini, cut in julienne strips
½ tsp. olive oil
⅛ tsp. garlic salt
⅛ tsp. white pepper

Place pecans on cookie sheet and toast in 350° oven; set aside.

Coat medium skillet with cooking spray. Add zucchini, olive oil, garlic salt, and pepper; sauté until tender.

Add pecans. Serve immediately.

SERVES: 2

Melange of Vegetables

1 Tbsp. olive oil

2 Tbsp. butter

1 leek, cut into julienne strips

3 carrots, cut into ¼-inch slices

3 small onions, thinly sliced

1½ cups red pepper, cut into strips

¼ cup chicken broth

Salt and pepper to taste

In skillet or wok, heat oil and butter; stir-fry leeks, carrots, onion, and red peppers for 2 minutes. Add chicken broth; salt and pepper. Stir well. Cover and simmer for 8 minutes, or until vegetables are tender.

SERVES: 6–8

Peacock Vegetables

1 red bell pepper,
seeded and cut
into strips

1 yellow bell pepper,
seeded and cut
into strips

1 green bell pepper,
seeded and cut
into strips

2 red onions, peeled
and cut into
wedges

2 small yellow
summer squash,
ends trimmed, cut
into ½-inch strips

2 small zucchini,
ends trimmed, cut
into ½-inch strips

4 garlic cloves,
peeled, thinly sliced

1 Tbsp. olive oil

1 tsp. dried oregano

2 Tbsp. fresh parsley,
minced

1 Tbsp. balsamic
vinegar

¼ tsp. salt

¼ tsp. pepper

 Prepare vegetables as directed and place in a large bowl.

In a small jar, combine oil, oregano, parsley, vinegar, salt, and pepper. Shake until well-combined. Pour over vegetables and toss to coat evenly.

Spread vegetables in a large roasting pan. Roast, uncovered, at 425° for 20 minutes; stir gently every 5 minutes.

Transfer to serving bowl. Adjust seasonings to taste.

NOTE: A good vegetable dish for tailgate parties or potluck dinners.

SERVES: 6

Missouri Vegetable Casserole

2 Tbsp. butter or margarine

½ cup onion, chopped

1 cup carrots, chopped

2 cups broccoli flowerets

1 medium bell pepper, chopped

2 cloves garlic, minced

1 cup long grain rice

1½ cups chicken broth

1 Tbsp. parsley, chopped

Salt and pepper to taste

1 cup Cheddar cheese, grated

Melt butter in a 2-quart sauce pan; sauté onion until tender. Add carrots and cook over medium heat for 3 minutes.

Add broccoli, bell pepper, garlic, and rice to onion mixture; stir to blend. Add chicken broth; bring to a boil. Cover with tight-fitting lid; cook over low to medium heat for about 20 minutes, or until rice is done.

Add parsley; salt and pepper. Toss in the cheese with a fork. Do not mash the vegetables.

Transfer mixture to a casserole dish. Broil until slightly browned, about 10 minutes.

SERVES: 6

Vegetable Strata

4 (10 oz.) pkgs. frozen chopped broccoli

½ lb. mushrooms, sliced

6 Tbsp. butter, divided

½ cup mayonnaise

½ cup sour cream

½ cup Parmesan cheese, grated

1 (14 oz.) can artichoke hearts, drained and chopped

Salt and pepper to taste

3 tomatoes, skinned and sliced, ½-inch thick

½ cup seasoned bread crumbs

 Cook broccoli according to package directions; drain and set aside.

In a small skillet, sauté mushrooms in 2 tablespoons butter; set aside.

In a large mixing bowl, combine mayonnaise, sour cream, and Parmesan cheese. Gently stir in artichokes, broccoli, and mushrooms; salt and pepper.

Pour mixture into a greased 9x13-inch casserole dish. Place sliced tomatoes over vegetable mixture.

Melt remaining ¼ cup butter; stir in bread crumbs and sprinkle over casserole.

Bake at 325° for 20 minutes or until bubbly.

SERVES: 8–10

1948, Age 63

Mrs. Truman's Frozen Lemon Pie

2 eggs, separated
1/3 cup fresh lemon juice
1 tablespoon grated lemon rind
1 cup whipped cream
1/4 cup sugar
1/2 cup crumbled graham crackers

Beat egg yolks. Add lemon juice, rind and all, with two tablespoons of the sugar. Cook over low heat, stirring constantly. Cool.

Beat egg whites, add two more tablespoons of the sugar, fold into cooked mixture; then fold in whipped cream.

Line greased pie or refrigerator pan with graham cracker crumbs. Save some to sprinkle on top. Pour filling into pan and freeze.

Serves four.

ABOVE: Mrs. Truman cuts the cake at the Roosevelt Birthday Ball held in the East Room of the White House. The stars who attended the January 28, 1946, event included: Cesar Romero, Angela Lansbury and Van Johnson.

BELOW: First Lady Bess Truman is honored with a gift from the wives of the cabinet members during a luncheon at the home of former Secretary of State Dean Acheson on January 20, 1953.

Chinese Almond Cookies

1 cup sugar
1 cup margarine, softened
1 tsp. almond extract
1 egg
2¼ cups flour
½ tsp. baking soda
1 cup almonds, chopped

In a mixing bowl, cream sugar and margarine until light and fluffy. Add extract and egg; blend well. Combine flour and baking soda; add to dough. Mix well. Cover and refrigerate for 1 hour.

Shape dough into 1-inch balls; roll in almonds. Place 2 inches apart on ungreased cookie sheet. Flatten with bottom of drinking glass.

Bake at 325° for 13–18 minutes.

YIELD: 3–4 dozen

Sugar Cookies

3 cups flour, sifted
1½ tsp. baking powder
½ tsp. salt
1 cup sugar
1 cup butter, softened
1 egg, slightly beaten
3 Tbsp. heavy cream
1 tsp. vanilla
¼ tsp. nutmeg, optional

In a bowl, sift together the flour, baking powder, salt, and sugar; cut in butter. Add slightly beaten egg, cream, vanilla, and nutmeg; blend well.

Roll dough out on floured surface to ¼-inch thickness. Cut into desired shape and sprinkle with sugar.

Place on ungreased cookie sheet and bake at 400° for 5–8 minutes or until delicately browned.

YIELD: 5 dozen

Ginger Snaps

¾ cup shortening
1 cup sugar
¼ cup light molasses
1 egg
2 cups flour
2 tsp. soda
½ tsp. cloves
½ tsp. ginger
1 tsp. cinnamon
½ tsp. salt

In a saucepan, melt shortening over low heat. Remove from heat and let cool. Add sugar, molasses, and egg; beat well. Sift remaining ingredients and add to mixture; beat well.

Chill for several hours. Form into 1-inch balls and roll in granulated sugar. Place on greased cookie sheet, 2 inches apart.

Bake at 350° for 8 minutes.

YIELD: 2–3 dozen

Oatmeal Surprises

1¼ cups flour
1 tsp. baking soda
1 cup margarine, softened
¼ cup granulated sugar
¾ cup brown sugar, packed
1 (3½ oz.) pkg. instant vanilla or butterscotch pudding
2 eggs, room temperature, beaten
1 tsp. vanilla
1 (12 oz.) pkg. semisweet chocolate chips
3 cups quick oatmeal

In a small bowl, sift together the flour and baking soda; set aside.

Cream together margarine, sugars, and pudding mix. Stir in beaten eggs and vanilla.

Add flour mixture and stir until well-blended. Add chocolate chips and oatmeal; stir until evenly mixed. An additional ½ cup of oatmeal may be added if dough seems too moist.

Form the dough into 1-inch balls and place on lightly greased cookie sheets.

Bake at 375° for 10–12 minutes.

YIELD: 4 dozen

Morning Cookies

¼ cup margarine,
   softened

½ cup brown sugar,
   packed

¾ cup whole wheat
   flour

¾ cup applesauce
   or pumpkin

½ cup oats

⅓ cup wheat bran

¼ cup nonfat dry
   milk powder

1 egg white

½ tsp. baking soda

½ tsp. cinnamon

¼ tsp. baking powder

¼ tsp. salt

⅛ tsp. cloves

½ cup raisins or dates

¼ cup nuts, chopped

Cream margarine and brown sugar until well-blended. Stir in all other ingredients, except raisins and nuts.

Fold raisins and nuts into mixture. Drop by spoonful onto cookie sheet.

Bake at 375° for 10 minutes.

YIELD: 2–3 dozen

Monster Cookies

3 eggs
1 cup brown sugar, packed
1 cup granulated sugar
2 tsp. baking soda
½ cup margarine
1½ cups crunchy peanut butter
4½ cups quick oats
1 tsp. vanilla
¾ cup M&M's
¾ cup semisweet chocolate chips

In a large bowl, combine all ingredients, except the M&M's and chocolate chips; mix with an electric mixer. Use a wooden spoon to stir in the M&M's and chocolate chips.

Lightly grease hands and form mixture into 1-inch balls. Place on ungreased cookie sheet.

Bake at 350° for 8–10 minutes.

NOTE: These cookies freeze well.

YIELD: 5 dozen

Marbled Swirls

2 cups flour
½ tsp. baking powder
¼ tsp. salt
½ cup brown sugar, packed
½ cup granulated sugar
½ cup butter, softened
1 large egg
½ cup sour cream
1 tsp. vanilla
1 cup semisweet chocolate chips

 In a medium bowl, mix flour, baking powder, and salt; set aside.

In a large bowl, cream sugars with butter and beat until blended. Add egg, sour cream, and vanilla; mix at medium speed until fluffy, about 2 minutes. Gradually add flour mixture at low speed. Do not overmix.

Melt chocolate chips over double boiler or in microwave, stirring often, until smooth. Cool chocolate to lukewarm and pour over batter. Using a wooden spoon, gently fold chocolate into batter, being careful not to fully mix.

Drop by rounded tablespoons 2 inches apart on ungreased cookie sheet.

Bake at 300° for 23–25 minutes. For best results, cool on flat surface only.

YIELD: 2½ dozen

Sinfully Rich Cookies

2 oz. unsweetened
  chocolate

1¾ cups semisweet
  chocolate chips,
  divided

½ cup butter

2 large eggs

1 cup sugar

2 tsp. vanilla

1½ cups flour

½ cup white
  chocolate chips

¼ cup milk
  chocolate chips

In top of double boiler, melt unsweetened chocolate and ¾ cup semi-sweet chocolate chips, stirring often until smooth.

In a large bowl, blend chocolate mixture and butter on medium speed of electric mixer. Add eggs, sugar, and vanilla; beat until blended. Scrape bowl often.

To this mixture, add flour, remaining semisweet chips, white and milk chocolate chips; mix until well-blended. Refrigerate one hour.

Form refrigerated dough into 1½-inch balls. Coat cookie sheet with cooking spray and place balls 2 inches apart on sheet. With hand, flatten ball to ½-inch thickness.

Bake at 375° for 10–12 minutes. Transfer to cool, flat surface.

YIELD: 2½ dozen

Bourbon Balls

1 cup vanilla wafers, crushed

1 cup walnuts, finely chopped

1 cup powdered sugar

¼ cup bourbon whiskey

2 Tbsp. cocoa

1½ Tbsp. light corn syrup

Additional powdered sugar

In a medium bowl, combine crushed vanilla wafers, walnuts, powdered sugar, bourbon, cocoa, and corn syrup.

Dust hands with powdered sugar; roll mixture into small balls. Roll each ball in powdered sugar.

Store in a cool place until ready to serve.

YIELD: 3 – 4 dozen

Chocolate Mint Fudge

3 cups chocolate mint chips

1 (14 oz.) can sweetened condensed milk

⅓ cup powdered sugar

1 tsp. vanilla

1 cup nuts, chopped, optional

In a 2-quart bowl, microwave chocolate chips and condensed milk, uncovered, on HIGH for 2 minutes. Stir until smooth. Add sugar, vanilla, and nuts, if desired. Stir until well-blended.

Pour into a 9-inch square pan coated with cooking spray; spread evenly. Chill in freezer until not quite firm, about 45 – 60 minutes. Cut into 1-inch squares. Cover tightly and freeze until ready to serve.

NOTE: Substitute plain chocolate chips and add mint flavoring to taste, if chocolate mint chips are unavailable.

YIELD: 6½ dozen

Irresistible Brownies

4 oz. semisweet
 chocolate, broken
2 cups sugar
1 cup margarine,
 softened
4 eggs
1 tsp. vanilla
1 cup flour, sifted
⅛ tsp. salt
2 cups English
 walnuts, chopped

 Melt chocolate in double boiler; set aside.

Cream sugar and margarine until well-blended; beat in eggs, one at a time. Add vanilla, flour, and salt. Stir in nuts.

Swirl melted chocolate into batter, leaving a marble effect. Pour into greased and floured 9x13-inch metal pan. Place in cold oven.

Bake at 275° for 1 hour. Cool; cut into squares.

NOTE: May be frozen after baking.

YIELD: 2 dozen

Butterbrickle Brownies

½ cup butter
2 oz. unsweetened
 chocolate
1 cup sugar
2 eggs
¾ cup flour
1 tsp. vanilla
¾ cup almond
 brickle bits
1 (6 oz.) pkg.
 semisweet
 chocolate chips

In a heavy saucepan, melt butter and chocolate. Remove from heat; stir in sugar, eggs, flour, and vanilla.

Pour into 8x8-inch greased pan. Sprinkle top with almond brickle bits and follow with chocolate chips.

Bake at 350° for 30 minutes.

SERVES: 9

Apple Cake

For the Cake:
- ¼ cup shortening
- 1 cup sugar
- 1 egg
- 1 cup flour
- 1 tsp. baking soda
- 1 tsp. cinnamon
- ¼ tsp. salt
- 2 cups apples, peeled and chopped
- ½ cup raisins
- 1 cup nuts, chopped

For the Icing:
- 6 Tbsp. butter, melted
- ⅔ cup sugar
- ¼ cup heavy cream
- 1 cup moist coconut, shredded
- ½ tsp. vanilla

CAKE

In a large mixing bowl, cream shortening and sugar. Add egg and beat well. Blend in dry ingredients; add apples, raisins, and nuts. Pour into 8x8-inch greased pan.

Bake at 350° for 30–35 minutes.

ICING

In a medium bowl, blend melted butter, sugar, cream, coconut, and vanilla.

When cake comes out of oven, spread with icing immediately. Place cake under broiler until lightly browned.

SERVES: 8

Coconut Sour Cream Dream Cake

1 (18½ oz.) pkg.
  butter-flavored
  cake mix
2 cups sugar
1 (8 oz.) carton
  sour cream
1 (12 oz.) pkg.
  frozen coconut,
  thawed
1½ cups heavy
  cream, whipped

Prepare cake according to directions, making two 8-inch layers. Split cooled layers horizontally.

Blend together the sugar, sour cream, and coconut; chill. Spread all but one cup between layers. Blend remaining cup of the mixture with whipped cream; spread top and sides of cake.

Seal in an airtight container and refrigerate. Store for three days before cutting.

SERVES: 10–12

Gooey Butter Cake

1 (18½ oz.) pkg.
  cake mix, without
  pudding
½ cup margarine,
  melted
1 egg
1 (8 oz.) pkg. cream
  cheese, softened
2 eggs, slightly
  beaten
1 lb. box powdered
  sugar, divided

In a large mixing bowl, combine cake mix, margarine, and egg. Press mixture into a 9x13-inch greased baking dish.

In another mixing bowl, combine cream cheese, eggs, and powdered sugar; reserve ¼ cup powdered sugar. Spread over cake mixture.

Bake at 350° for 40 minutes. Sprinkle remaining powdered sugar on top.

NOTE: Delicious with strawberries!

SERVES: 10–12

Lemon Supreme Cake

For the Cake:

1 (18½ oz.) lemon
   cake mix, without
   pudding
⅓ cup sugar
¾ cup oil
1 cup apricot nectar
4 eggs, room
   temperature
½ cup pecans,
   chopped

For the Glaze:

1 cup powdered
   sugar
1½ lemons

 CAKE

In a large bowl, combine cake mix, sugar, oil and apricot nectar, beating well. Add eggs, one at a time, beating well after each addition.

Spray bundt pan with vegetable spray. Place pecans in bottom of pan; pour batter over nuts.

Bake at 325° for 1 hour.

GLAZE

In a small bowl, combine powdered sugar and juice of lemons to make glaze. Brush mixture over cake while still warm, brushing three times.

SERVES: 16

Strawberry Cake

For the Cake:

1 (18 ½ oz.) pkg.
white cake mix

1 (3 oz.) pkg.
strawberry gelatin

⅔ cup vegetable oil

4 eggs

1 cup frozen
strawberries,
thawed and
crushed

½ cup nuts, chopped,
optional

For the Icing:

4 Tbsp. butter, melted

2 cups powdered
sugar

2 Tbsp. juice from
frozen strawberries

CAKE

In a large bowl, combine cake mix, gelatin, oil, and eggs. Beat well after adding each egg.

Mix in strawberries, saving 2 tablespoons strawberry juice for icing. Add nuts, if desired.

Pour batter into greased and floured bundt pan.

Bake at 350° for 30–45 minutes.

ICING

In a saucepan, melt butter and mix with powdered sugar. Stir until smooth.

Add just enough of the strawberry juice to make the consistency thin enough to drizzle over cake that is completely cooled.

SERVES: 16

Graham Torte

For the Torte:
½ cup shortening
1 cup sugar
2 eggs, beaten
1 cup flour
2 tsp. baking powder
¼ tsp. salt
1 cup graham
   cracker crumbs
1 cup milk
1 tsp. vanilla

For the Filling:
⅓ cup sugar
3 Tbsp. cornstarch
¼ tsp. salt
2 cups milk
2 egg yolks
2 Tbsp. butter
1 tsp. vanilla
   Whipped cream

 TORTE

Cream together shortening and sugar. Add the beaten eggs to sugar mixture. Mix in flour, baking powder, and salt.

Alternately add the graham cracker crumbs and milk. Add vanilla; pour into two greased and floured 8-inch cake pans.

Bake at 350° for 25 minutes. After the cakes have cooled, slice horizontally to make 4 layers.

FILLING

In a heavy pan, combine sugar, cornstarch, and salt. Add milk; heat slowly until thickened. Stir ¼ cup milk mixture into egg yolks; slowly incorporate back into hot liquid, beating constantly until well-blended. Add butter and vanilla. Cover and refrigerate.

To assemble, stack layers with one-fourth filling between each. Top with remaining filling and whipped cream.

SERVES: 12

Chocolate Buttermilk Cake

For the Cake:
2½ cups cake flour
½ cup cocoa
2 tsp. baking soda
¾ tsp. salt
2¼ cups sugar
1 cup unsalted butter, softened
2 large eggs
1 tsp. vanilla
2 cups buttermilk

For the Frosting:
1⅓ cups sugar
1 cup whipping cream
5½ oz. unsweetened chocolate, cut into small pieces
½ cup butter, softened
1 Tbsp. vanilla

 CAKE

In a medium mixing bowl, sift flour, cocoa, soda, and salt together; set aside.

In a large mixing bowl, cream sugar and butter; mix on high for three minutes. Add eggs, one at a time, beating well. Add vanilla.

To the cream mixture, alternately add a third of the dry ingredients and half the buttermilk, beginning and ending with dry ingredients; blend. Pour into three 9-inch round cake pans lined with buttered wax paper.

Bake at 350° for 30 minutes. Cool in pans 5 minutes. Loosen with knife and invert on wire rack. When cool, spread with frosting.

FROSTING

In a heavy 3-quart pan, combine sugar and cream; heat, stirring to dissolve. Bring to a boil and cook an additional 6 minutes.

Remove from heat; add chocolate and butter, stirring until melted. Add vanilla.

Refrigerate until well-chilled, but not solid. Stir vigorously with wooden spoon until soft and spreadable.

SERVES: 12

Mint Bon Bon Cake

For the Cake:

1 cup peppermint, chocolate chip or mint chip ice cream

⅓ cup margarine, softened

½ cup sugar

1 egg

1½ cups flour

2¼ tsp. baking powder

½ tsp. baking soda

¼ tsp. salt

1 cup buttermilk

1 tsp. peppermint extract

Green food coloring, optional

⅔ cup fudge ice cream topping

For the Frosting:

2½ Tbsp. flour

½ cup milk

½ cup sugar

½ cup butter, softened

1 tsp. peppermint extract

Green food coloring

Shaved chocolate for topping

 CAKE

Measure ice cream by packing firmly into cup and leveling off. Soften at room temperature.

In a large mixing bowl, cream margarine and sugar; add egg, beat until smooth. Add flour, baking powder, baking soda, salt, buttermilk, peppermint extract, 2–3 drops food coloring, and softened ice cream. Beat at low speed until well-blended. Pour into well-greased and lightly floured 8-inch square pan.

Bake at 350° for 35–40 minutes, until top springs back when touched lightly in center. Cool 10 minutes; remove from pan. When completely cooled, place on serving plate. Spread sides and top with fudge topping.

FROSTING

In a small saucepan, combine flour and milk. Cook over medium heat until mixture is very thick, stirring constantly. Cool completely.

In a small mixing bowl, beat sugar and butter until light and fluffy. Gradually add flour mixture. Continue beating at high speed until the consistency of whipped cream. Blend in peppermint extract and food coloring.

Frost fudge-covered cake with peppermint frosting. Garnish with shaved chocolate. Refrigerate until served.

SERVES: 12

Chocolate Raspberry Torte

For the Cake:

- 3 oz. unsweetened chocolate
- ½ cup butter or margarine, softened
- 2½ cups light brown sugar, packed
- 3 eggs
- 1 tsp. vanilla
- 2 tsp. baking soda
- ½ tsp. salt
- 2 cups flour
- 1 (8 oz.) carton sour cream
- 1 cup water

CAKE

In a saucepan, melt unsweetened chocolate; set aside to cool. In a large mixing bowl, beat butter or margarine with electric mixer at high speed for 30 seconds. Add brown sugar and eggs. Beat until light and fluffy. Beat in vanilla, cooled chocolate, baking soda, and salt.

Add flour to batter alternately with sour cream, beating after each addition to combine. Pour in water; beat on low speed until blended. Divide the batter between 2 greased and floured 9-inch round baking pans.

Bake at 350° for 40–45 minutes or until toothpick inserted in the center comes out clean.

Cool cakes in pans on wire racks for 10 minutes. Remove cakes from the pans. Cool thoroughly on wire racks.

For the Frosting:

1½ cups unsalted butter, softened

8 cups sifted powdered sugar, divided

½ cup cocoa

½ cup whipping cream

¼ cup red raspberry liqueur

For the Assembly:

½ cup seedless red raspberry preserves

½ cup red raspberry liqueur

FROSTING

In a large mixing bowl, beat butter on high speed for 30 seconds. Reduce to low speed; beat in 2 cups powdered sugar and cocoa. Add cream and liqueur; beat well. Beat in enough sifted powdered sugar, about 6 cups, to make a fluffy frosting.

ASSEMBLY

Heat red raspberry preserves until easy to spread.

Split each cooled cake in half horizontally, forming 4 layers. Place 1 layer, cut side up, on a serving plate. Sprinkle with 2 tablespoons liqueur. Spread with about 2½ tablespoons raspberry preserves. Then, carefully spread with ⅔ cup frosting.

Place a second layer on top of frosted layer, cut side down. Use a fork to poke holes in crust of cake. Drizzle with liqueur; spread with jam and frosting as before. Repeat with third layer, placing cut side up, using 2 tablespoons liqueur, remaining preserves and ⅔ cup frosting. Top with fourth layer, cut side down. Poke holes and drizzle with the remaining liqueur.

Frost top and sides of cake with remaining frosting. If desired, pipe any remaining frosting onto cake to garnish. Store the finished cake, covered, in refrigerator. Serve chilled.

SERVES: 12

Chocolate Mousse Roll

For the Filling:
1½ cups semisweet
   chocolate chips
⅓ cup sugar
¼ cup water
3 eggs, separated
2 tsp. vanilla extract

FILLING

In the top of double boiler, melt chocolate chips and sugar in water; stir until smooth. Remove from heat and cool.

Beat egg yolks until thick and lemon-colored; add to chocolate. Stir in vanilla extract.

Beat egg whites until stiff. Fold into chocolate mixture and whisk until whites are incorporated. Refrigerate 3–4 hours.

NOTE: Sweetened whipped cream or flavored ice cream is a nice alternative for the filling.

For the Cake:
- 6 Tbsp. cocoa
- 6 Tbsp. cake flour
- ¼ tsp. salt
- ¾ tsp. baking powder
- 4 eggs, separated
- ¾ cup sugar
- 1 tsp. vanilla extract
  Powdered sugar, for garnish

CAKE

Sift together cocoa, flour, salt, and baking powder; set aside.

Beat egg whites until soft peaks form. Mix in sugar, 1 tablespoon at a time.

Beat yolks until very thick; add vanilla extract. Gently fold egg whites into yolks. Fold into dry ingredients, just until well-blended.

Grease a 10x15-inch jelly roll pan and line with wax paper that has been greased. Spread batter evenly in pan. Cake will be thin.

Bake at 400° for 10–13 minutes. Turn out on towel sprinkled with powdered sugar. Cut off hard edges. Roll up in towel and cool completely.

Unroll cooled cake and spread with chilled mousse filling. Roll up and slice.

SERVES: 10

Chocolate Love

For the Truffles:
- ¼ cup whipping cream
- 2 oz. semisweet chocolate, chopped

For the Cake:
- 4 oz. semisweet chocolate
- 1½ oz. unsweetened chocolate
- ½ cup plus 3 Tbsp. unsalted butter
- 3 large eggs, room temperature
- 3 large egg yolks, room temperature
- ⅓ cup sugar
- ⅓ cup flour

 TRUFFLES

Heat cream to boiling in small saucepan. Remove from heat. Add chopped chocolate; stir until melted and smooth; cool 10 minutes. On sheet of wax paper, shape mixture into 8-inch log. Wrap and refrigerate 3 hours or freeze 2 hours, until firm. Cut into 8 equal pieces.

NOTE: These can be made ahead. Wrap and refrigerate up to 24 hours.

CAKE

Melt chocolates with butter in medium microwave-proof bowl on HIGH for 2 minutes; stir until completely melted and smooth. Cool to room temperature.

Butter and lightly flour eight 6-ounce custard cups. Place on cookie sheet.

In mixer bowl, combine eggs, egg yolks, and sugar. Beat at high speed until mixture is thick and forms a ribbon when beaters are lifted, 8–10 minutes. Sift flour over mixture and fold in gently. Fold in cooled chocolate-butter mixture in 2 batches. Pour batter into prepared custard cups.

For the Garnish:

1 Tbsp. powdered
   sugar
Fresh raspberries

Bake at 400° for 5 minutes. Remove from oven. With spoon, quickly place one truffle on center of each cake (truffle will sink). Return to oven and bake 4–5 minutes more, until tops of cakes are dry and begin to pull away from sides of cups. Cool in cups on wire rack for 5 minutes.

With small sharp knife, carefully loosen cakes from cups and invert onto 8 dessert plates.

GARNISH

Sift powdered sugar lightly over tops. Serve warm with whipped cream or ice cream and fresh raspberries.

NOTE: Chocolate can be melted in a double boiler over simmering water, stirring occasionally, rather than in the microwave.

SERVES: 8

Frozen Chocolate Velvet

2 cups whipping cream

⅔ cup sweetened condensed milk

⅔ cup chocolate syrup

¼ cup Amaretto or Kahlua, optional

¼ cup strong coffee, optional

1 cup almonds, sliced and toasted for garnish

In a medium mixing bowl, whip the cream until soft peaks form. Combine sweetened milk and chocolate syrup; fold into whipped cream, mixing until color is consistent. Fold in liqueur and/or coffee, if desired.

Spoon mixture into paper-lined muffin tins. Garnish with almonds. Freeze until ready to serve.

SERVES: 8–12

Sweetened Condensed Milk

¾ cup sugar

⅓ cup water

¼ cup butter

1 cup dry milk crystals

In a 2-cup glass measuring cup, add sugar, water, and butter. Microwave on HIGH 1½–2 minutes until mixture boils, stirring every 30 seconds.

Put mixture in a blender and combine with dry milk. Process until smooth. Refrigerate until needed.

YIELD: 1 cup

Simple Spumoni

2 cups whipping cream

⅔ cup sweetened condensed milk

½ tsp. rum extract

1 (20 oz.) can cherry pie filling

½ cup almonds, chopped

½ cup miniature chocolate chips

In a large bowl, combine whipping cream, condensed milk, and rum extract; cover and refrigerate for 30 minutes.

Remove from refrigerator and beat just until soft peaks form. Do not overbeat.

Fold in cherry pie filling, almonds, and chocolate chips. Transfer to an 8-inch square pan.

Cover and freeze about 4 hours, until firm.

SERVES: 12

Crunchy Snowballs

¾ cup slivered
  almonds, toasted
¾ cup shredded
  coconut, toasted
1 pt. ice cream—
  vanilla, strawberry
  or chocolate

 In a medium bowl, combine toasted almonds and coconut.

Scoop ice cream into 6 balls; roll each in almond-coconut mixture, pressing to coat.

Freeze firm. Store up to a week covered with foil or plastic wrap. Serve frozen, topped with favorite sauce.

SERVES: 6

Hot Fudge

½ cup butter
4 oz. unsweetened
  chocolate
3 cups sugar
½ tsp. salt
1 (12 oz.) can
  evaporated milk

Melt butter in double boiler; add chocolate and melt. Add sugar slowly, stirring constantly until well-blended. Add salt and milk; cook until hot and smooth.

NOTE: Sauce can be frozen and used as needed.

YIELD: 4 cups

Butterscotch

¼ cup butter
½ cup brown sugar,
  packed
½ cup light cream

Melt butter in small saucepan. Stir in brown sugar until dissolved. Gradually add the light cream. Cook over low heat until smooth, about 3 minutes.

NOTE: Sauce can be frozen and used as needed.

YIELD: 1 cup

Raisin Sundae Pie

For the Crust:
1 egg white
¼ tsp. salt
¼ cup sugar
1½ cups walnuts, chopped
Butter or margarine

For the Filling:
1 pt. coffee ice cream, softened
1 pt. vanilla ice cream, softened

For the Sauce:
½ cup golden raisins
3 Tbsp. butter
1 cup brown sugar, packed
½ cup half & half
1 tsp. vanilla

 CRUST

Place egg white and salt in bowl and beat until stiff, but not dry; gradually beat in sugar. Fold in walnuts. Turn into well-buttered 9-inch pie plate. With spoon, spread evenly on bottom and sides of dish.

Bake at 400° for 10–12 minutes.
Cool and refrigerate.

FILLING

Fill cooled crust with layers of coffee and vanilla ice cream. Freeze until firm. Serve with raisin caramel sauce.

SAUCE

Chop the raisins coarsely. Combine butter and brown sugar in a saucepan. Cook, stirring until sugar is melted and lightly browned.

Remove from heat; slowly stir in half & half and raisins. Heat 1 minute longer; stir in vanilla. Serve warm or cold over pie.

SERVES: 8–10

Mocha Baked Alaska

For the Brownies:
½ recipe Irresistible
Brownies (p. 322)

For the Mold:
1 qt. chocolate
ice cream
1 qt. coffee ice cream

For the Meringue:
5 egg whites,
(about ⅔ cup)
⅔ cup sugar

BROWNIES

Prepare the brownie recipe as directed except, instead of swirling, mix chocolate into other ingredients.

Bake in one 8-inch round cake pan at 275° for 45 minutes. For each Baked Alaska, you will use only one pan. Cool brownie layer. Remove from pan and place layer in freezer.

MOLD

Line a 1½-quart, 8-inch diameter, dome-shaped mixing bowl with aluminum foil; allow 1 inch extra foil to extend over edge of bowl.

Stir chocolate ice cream to soften slightly. Spread a layer about 1 inch thick, to cover bottom and sides of foil-lined mold. Place mold in freezer. Stir coffee ice cream to soften. When chocolate layer is firm, pack coffee ice cream into center of mold; smooth top; freeze firm. Cover with foil.

Let mold of ice cream stand at room temperature while making the meringue.

MERINGUE

To prepare the meringue, beat egg whites until soft peaks form; gradually add sugar, beating to stiff peaks. Set aside.

Baked Alaska,
continued

BAKED ALASKA

Remove foil from top of ice cream. Place frozen brownie layer on top of mold. Place a cookie sheet on top of brownie layer and invert. Unmold and peel off foil.

Quickly cover ice cream and brownie base with meringue, making sure all areas of ice cream and brownie are covered.

Bake at 500° on lowest rack for 3–5 minutes or until meringue is browned.

Let stand a few minutes for easier cutting. Cut in wedge-shaped slices.

NOTE: This is an ideal recipe to freeze up to 2 days ahead. The completed Baked Alaska can be frozen, including the meringue.

• This recipe can also be made using a light brownie mix and frozen yogurts such as raspberry or orange flavors.

SERVES: 12

Creamy Bombé with Raspberry Sauce

For the Bombé:

1 (16 oz.) pkg.
  frozen unsweetened
  sliced peaches,
  thawed and
  drained
1 (8 oz.) carton sour
  cream
½ cup grenadine
½ gal. vanilla ice
  cream, softened
  Fresh raspberries,
  optional
  Fresh mint sprigs,
  optional

For the Sauce:

1 (16 oz.) pkg.
  frozen unsweetened
  raspberries,
  thawed and
  undrained
¾ cup light corn
  syrup
¼ cup Grand Marnier

BOMBÉ

Blend peaches in food processor until smooth. Add sour cream and grenadine; process until well-blended.

In a large mixing bowl, combine peach mixture and ice cream. Beat with electric mixer, on low speed, until well-blended. Pour mixture into an 11-cup mold that has been coated with cooking spray. Cover and freeze 8 hours or until firm.

Two hours before serving, loosen edges of ice cream from mold. Invert mold onto a chilled serving plate. Wrap a warm towel around mold for 30 seconds. Shake gently and slowly lift off mold. Return bombé immediately to freezer.

If desired, garnish with raspberries and mint. To serve, cut bombé into slices and top with raspberry sauce.

SAUCE

Purée raspberries in food processor. Strain raspberries and discard seeds. Stir in syrup and Grand Marnier.

SERVES: 12

Lite Sour Cream Cheesecake

1 envelope
  unflavored gelatin
¼ cup cold water
¾ cup boiling water
1 (8 oz.) carton lite
  sour cream
1 (8 oz.) pkg. lite
  cream cheese,
  softened
½ cup sugar
1 tsp. vanilla extract
¾ cup graham
  cracker crumbs
2 Tbsp. margarine,
  melted
  Blueberries
  Strawberries
  Kiwi

In a blender, sprinkle unflavored gelatin over cold water; let stand 2 minutes. Add boiling water and process at low speed until gelatin is completely dissolved, about 2 minutes.

Add next four ingredients; process at high speed until blended, about 2 minutes.

In a 9-inch pie plate, mix graham cracker crumbs and melted margarine. Press evenly over bottom and up sides.

Fill crust with cheese mixture. Chill until firm, about 4 hours.

Decorate with an outer band of blueberries, a middle band of sliced strawberries, and an inner band of sliced kiwi. Leave center undecorated.

SERVES: 8

Black and White Bars

For the Crust:

- 1 (8½ oz.) pkg. chocolate sandwich cookies, (Oreos)
- 8 Tbsp. unsalted butter, divided
- 1 Tbsp. sugar

For the Filling:

- 10 oz. white chocolate
- ½ cup whipping cream
- 2 (8 oz.) pkgs. cream cheese
- 4 large eggs, separated
- 4 tsp. vanilla
- ⅛ tsp. salt

 CRUST

Line the bottom and sides of 9x13-inch baking pan with heavy-duty aluminum foil. Coat the foil with 2 tablespoons melted butter.

Crush chocolate wafer cookies into crumbs; reserve a small amount for garnish. Add remaining butter and sugar. Press crumb mixture evenly over bottom of foil-lined pan.

FILLING

In a double boiler, melt chocolate. Pour into a mixing bowl; set double boiler aside for later use. Gradually stir cream into melted chocolate. Set aside to cool slightly.

Beat the cream cheese until smooth. Beat in egg yolks, one at a time, scraping side of bowl frequently with a spatula.

Add chocolate mixture, vanilla, and salt. Beat filling for 2 minutes.

Using clean beaters and bowl, beat egg whites to firm peaks and fold into chocolate mixture. Pour filling evenly over crust.

Bake at 300° for 30 minutes on middle rack until filling has risen and is almost set. Turn off heat, leaving pan in the oven for 30 minutes. Cool to room temperature.

For the Topping:
   6 oz. white chocolate
   ¼ cup whipping
      cream
   2 Tbsp. white crème
      de cacao

TOPPING

Reheat water in double boiler; melt chocolate. Gradually stir in cream and crème de cacao. Pour the white chocolate topping over cooled cheesecake. When cool, cover and freeze the bars for 2 hours.

Using the foil corners as handles, lift the frozen cheesecake from the pan and set on a flat surface. With a large knife dipped in very hot water, cut the frozen cheesecake into 1½-inch squares. Keep bars frozen until ready to garnish.

Top bars with reserved crumbs. Drizzle with melted semisweet chocolate, or with semisweet chocolate curls. Serve immediately or store in refrigerator and serve chilled.

NOTE: May be frozen for up to one month before garnishing.

YIELD: 48 bars

White Chocolate Fruit Tart

For the Pastry:

- 2 oz. white chocolate
  Grated zest of one orange
- ¼ cup granulated sugar
- ¾ cup unsalted butter
- 1 Tbsp. powdered sugar
- ⅛ tsp. salt
- 2 cups flour

For the Filling:

- 1 cup whipping cream, divided
- 6 oz. white chocolate
- 1 Tbsp. granulated sugar
- 1 Tbsp. orange liqueur or undiluted frozen orange juice

PASTRY

Finely chop white chocolate with knife or in food processor; reserve.

In food processor, mince orange zest with granulated sugar until zest is fine as the sugar.

Melt butter in a saucepan over medium heat. Remove from heat; stir in powdered sugar and orange zest. Add salt and flour; stir well. Cool enough to handle, as dough must be worked with before it has cooled completely.

Place dough in a 10-inch tart pan with removable bottom. Press dough out evenly over bottom and up sides of pan. Placing plastic wrap over dough makes it easier to spread. Chill 30 minutes.

Bake at 350° for 15 minutes until golden brown. Remove from oven and sprinkle with white chocolate. Using the back of a spoon, spread chocolate over bottom and sides of shell; chill.

FILLING

In a saucepan, heat ¼-cup whipping cream to a simmer. Chop the chocolate and stir into the hot cream until it is melted and smooth; cool.

Whip remaining cream, sugar, and liqueur until stiff. Fold into cooled chocolate mixture; spoon into the pastry. Refrigerate until set. Filling can be prepared 1 day ahead.

For the Glaze:

½ cup seedless all-
fruit raspberry jam

1 Tbsp. orange
liqueur or
undiluted frozen
orange juice

For the Garnish:

Strawberries,
halved

Raspberries

Peaches, sliced

Nectarines, sliced

Mangoes, sliced

Kiwi, sliced

GLAZE

In a small bowl, stir jam and orange liqueur together. Brush thin layer over set white chocolate filling. Set remainder aside to brush fruit with at the end.

GARNISH

Select two or more of the fruits and arrange in decorative pattern on top of tart. Brush with glaze. Serve chilled.

SERVES: 10

Flan

1 cup sugar
4 whole eggs, beaten
2 egg yolks
½ cup sugar
1 tsp. vanilla
¼ tsp. salt
1½ cups cream,
    whipped
1½ cups whole milk

Heat 1 cup sugar in pan until medium brown, caramelizing syrup. Remove immediately and divide into 6 custard cups. Rotate each cup to slightly coat bottom; cool.

Combine whole eggs, yolks, sugar, vanilla, and salt; blend.

Place cream and milk in pan and heat to boiling point. Remove from heat and slowly add to egg mixture, stirring constantly to avoid cooking eggs.

Divide mixture equally into custard cups. Place cups in shallow baking pan filled with 1 inch boiling water.

Bake at 325° for 40–45 minutes or until toothpick comes out clean. If top begins to brown, cover with foil. Do not overcook.

Refrigerate at least 6 hours before serving.

SERVES: 6

Danish Pastry Bar

For the Pastry:
2½ cups flour
1 tsp. salt
1 cup shortening
1 egg, separated
　Enough milk
　added to egg yolk
　to make ⅔ cup

For the Filling:
½ cup corn flakes,
　crushed
10 apples, pared and
　sliced
1 cup sugar
1½ tsp. cinnamon

For the Glaze:
1 cup powdered
　sugar
1 Tbsp. water
1 Tbsp. vanilla

PASTRY

In a medium bowl, blend together the flour, salt, and shortening. Add the egg yolk, reserving egg white and milk mixture; stir until dough forms. Roll out half of pastry dough and place on a greased cookie sheet or jelly roll pan.

FILLING

Sprinkle crushed corn flakes on the pastry. Place the sliced apples on top of corn flakes. Sprinkle sugar and cinnamon over apples.

Roll out other half of dough to fit over the pastry filled with apples. Pinch dough together as you would a pie crust and seal with egg white, mixed with 1 tablespoon water.

Sprinkle top lightly with sugar.

Bake at 375° for 30 minutes or until pastry is slightly browned.

NOTE: A 21-ounce can of apple pie filling may be substituted for the apples.

GLAZE

In a medium bowl, combine powdered sugar, water, and vanilla. Drizzle over warm pastry.

SERVES: 16

Cherry Shortcake Squares

1 cup butter
1½ cups sugar
4 eggs, beaten
2 cups flour
1 tsp. vanilla extract
1 tsp. lemon extract
1 (21 oz.) can cherry pie filling
Powdered sugar

In a large mixing bowl, cream together butter and sugar. Add eggs and flour; mix in extracts.

Spread batter in greased 15½x10½x1-inch pan. Cut surface of batter into 28 squares. Spoon pie filling in center of each square. Batter will puff up during baking.

Bake at 350° for 45 minutes, or until golden brown; cut into squares. Sprinkle squares with powdered sugar.

SERVES: 28

Easy Fruit Cobbler

½ cup sugar
1 Tbsp. cornstarch
4 cups fruit, fresh or frozen, dry packed
2 Tbsp. water
1 cup biscuit mix
¼ cup milk
1 Tbsp. sugar
1 Tbsp. butter
¼ cup pecans, chopped, optional
Sugar for topping

In a large saucepan, mix the sugar and cornstarch. Add fruit and water. Stir and bring to a boil. Cook 1 minute longer. Pour into 1½-quart casserole.

In a small bowl, combine biscuit mix, milk, sugar, butter, and pecans. Stir until soft dough forms. Drop by spoonfuls on top of hot fruit. Sprinkle with sugar.

Bake at 425° for 15 minutes.

NOTE: Canned fruit may be used, but use water-packed fruit or decrease sugar in recipe. May use peaches, blueberries, blackberries, or any combination.

SERVES: 6

Topsy-Turvy Apple Pie

5 Tbsp. butter,
  divided

½ cup pecan halves

½ cup light brown
  sugar, firmly
  packed

2 (9-inch) unbaked
  pie crusts

8 medium apples,
  peeled, cored, and
  sliced

2 Tbsp. lemon juice

1 Tbsp. flour

1 cup granulated
  sugar

½ cup dark brown
  sugar, firmly
  packed

1 tsp. cinnamon

½ tsp. nutmeg

1 tsp. vanilla

1 Tbsp. cornstarch

Melt 4 tablespoons butter in 9-inch deep-dish pie plate; tilt and swirl to coat sides. Place pecans on bottom of pie plate in a pattern, rounded side down. Pat light brown sugar evenly over pecans and butter. Cover with one pastry layer.

Mix apple slices, lemon juice, flour, granulated sugar, dark brown sugar, cinnamon, nutmeg, vanilla, and cornstarch; spoon into pie plate. Dot with remaining tablespoon butter.

Fit top pastry over filling; flute edges, and cut slits in top to vent steam. Moisten the edges slightly with water.

Bake at 350° for 45–50 minutes. Remove from oven. Cool on a wire rack for 5–10 minutes before turning pie out onto a large plate.

NOTE: This rich-tasting pie can be served hot or cold. Use whipped cream or ice cream as an accompaniment.

SERVES: 8

China Clipper Pie

For the Pie:
- 1 cup sugar
- ½ tsp. ginger
- 1 tsp. cinnamon
- ¼ tsp. nutmeg
- ¼ tsp. salt
- 2 Tbsp. flour
- 3 Tbsp. strong tea
- 1 Tbsp. lemon juice
- 6 cups apples, thinly sliced
- 1 (9-inch) unbaked pie shell

For the Topping:
- ½ cup margarine
- ½ cup sugar
- ½ cup flour

 PIE

In a large bowl, combine sugar, ginger, cinnamon, nutmeg, salt, flour, tea, lemon juice, and sliced apples. Pour into pie shell.

TOPPING

In a mixing bowl, combine the margarine, sugar, and flour. Sprinkle on top of apples.

Bake at 400° for 55–60 minutes.

NOTE: This pie can be frozen unbaked. When ready to bake, place frozen pie in the oven and bake at 350° for 1½–2 hours.

- May use regular pastry for top.
- To keep the crust from over-browning, put aluminum foil on crust edge during baking.

SERVES: 8

Mile-High Raspberry Pie

1 cup sugar

2 egg whites

1 (12 oz.) bag frozen raspberries

1 tsp. vanilla

1 Tbsp. lemon juice

⅛ tsp. salt

1 cup whipping cream, whipped

1 (9-inch) baked pie shell

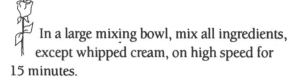 In a large mixing bowl, mix all ingredients, except whipped cream, on high speed for 15 minutes.

Fold whipped cream into mixture; pour into pie shell. Freeze overnight. May be frozen several days in advance of serving.

Before serving, place in refrigerator 20 minutes.

NOTE: For a spectacular presentation, top with Hot Fudge (see page 338).

SERVES: 8-10

Fresh Strawberry Pie

1 (10 oz.) carton
    frozen strawberries
1 cup sugar
3 Tbsp. cornstarch
    Red food coloring,
    optional
1½ qts. fresh
    strawberries,
    hulled
    Pastry dough for 1
    (9-inch) pie crust
¼ cup pecans,
    finely chopped

Thaw and strain frozen strawberries over colander. To the juice, add enough water to make 1½ cups.

In a saucepan, combine sugar and cornstarch; slowly add the juice and cook until thickened, stirring constantly. Cool and add food coloring if desired. Fold in berries.

Make dough for crust, adding the finely chopped pecans in the dough mixture. Roll out crust; line pie pan and crimp edge.

Bake at 425° for 15 minutes. Cool completely and fill with berry mixture.

NOTE: Can garnish with whipped cream.

SERVES: 8

Kiwi Lime Pie

For the Crust:
- 2 cups flour
- 1 tsp. salt
- ⅔ cup shortening
- 7 Tbsp. water, divided

 CRUST

Combine flour and salt; cut in shortening. Sprinkle 1 tablespoon water over part of mixture; toss with fork and push to side of bowl. Repeat with remaining tablespoons water until all is moistened. Form dough into ball.

On a floured surface, roll half the pastry into a 12-inch circle. Line a 9-inch pie plate with pastry. Trim and flute edge; prick pastry.

Bake at 450° for 10–12 minutes. Cool.

Divide remaining pastry in half. Roll each half into circles ⅛-inch thick; cut an 8¾-inch circle out of one portion and an 8-inch circle out of the other.

Place on baking sheet; prick and bake at 450° for 10 minutes. Cool; set aside.

For the Filling:

¾ *cup sugar*

⅓ *cup flour*

⅛ *tsp. salt*

1¾ *cups milk*

3 *eggs, beaten*

¼ *cup margarine
or butter*

2 *tsp. lime peel,
finely grated*

¼ *cup lime juice*

1 *(8 oz.) carton
lemon yogurt*

*Few drops green
food coloring*

¼ *cup apple jelly*

Whipped cream

2 *limes, sliced*

2 *kiwi fruit, peeled
and sliced*

FILLING

In a saucepan, combine sugar, flour, and salt; stir in milk. Stir over medium heat until bubbly. Reduce heat; cook and stir 2 minutes more. Remove from heat; stir 1 cup hot mixture into eggs. Return to saucepan; cook and stir until thickened. Cook and stir 2 minutes more. Do not boil. Remove from heat. Stir in margarine, lime peel, and juice. Fold in yogurt. Tint with few drops food coloring. Cover surface with plastic wrap and let cool.

Brush pie shell with some jelly. Place about 1 cup custard in shell. Cover with 8-inch pastry; brush with jelly. Spread with 1¼ cups custard. Top with 8¾-inch pastry; brush with jelly and top with remaining custard. Cover and chill overnight.

To serve pie, garnish with whipped cream, lime, and kiwi.

SERVES: 8–10

Variations on a Lemon Pie

For the Buttercrunch Crust:

1 cup flour
½ cup butter
½ cup coconut
⅓ cup nuts, chopped

For the Pink Cream Filling

8 oz. cream cheese
1 (14 oz.) can sweetened condensed milk
1 (6 oz.) can pink lemonade concentrate, thawed
    Red food coloring, optional
1 cup heavy cream, stiffly whipped

 CRUST

In a medium bowl, combine ingredients; spread out on a shallow baking pan. Bake at 350° for 15–20 minutes until light brown; stir frequently to break up pieces.

Press crust mixture into 9-inch pie pan while still hot, reserving some of the mixture for topping. Let shell cool.

NOTE: One of the following three lemon pie fillings may be used with this crust.

PINK CREAM FILLING

In a large bowl, beat cream cheese until fluffy. Beat in milk, lemonade, and a few drops of food coloring. Fold in whipped cream. Chill for 30 minutes. Pour into prepared crust.

Freeze until firm. Remove 10 minutes before serving.

For Chiffon Filling:

1 cup sugar, divided
1 envelope
  unflavored gelatin
⅔ cup water
⅓ cup lemon juice
4 eggs, separated
1 Tbsp. lemon rind,
  grated
½ tsp. cream of tartar
  Whipped cream

For Ice Cream Filling

1 qt. vanilla ice
  cream, softened
1 (6 oz.) can frozen
  lemonade, thawed

CHIFFON FILLING

In a saucepan, blend ½ cup sugar, gelatin, water, lemon juice, and beaten egg yolks thoroughly. Cook over medium heat, stirring constantly, just until mixture comes to a boil; stir in lemon rind. Place pan in ice water; cool until mixture mounds slightly when dropped from a spoon.

In a large bowl, beat egg whites with cream of tartar until frothy; gradually add ½ cup sugar. Beat until stiff and glossy. Carefully fold meringue into lemon filling.

Pile into the pie shell. Chill several hours. Serve with whipped cream, if desired.

ICE CREAM FILLING

In a medium bowl, combine softened ice cream with lemonade, place in pie shell and freeze.

SERVES: 8

Angel Lite Fruit Dip

1 (8 oz.) lite cream
  cheese, softened
½ tsp. ground
  cinnamon
¼ tsp. ground nutmeg
1 (7 oz.) jar
  marshmallow
  cream

 In a small bowl, blend cinnamon and nutmeg into cream cheese. Fold marshmallow cream into cream cheese mixture.

Serve with fresh fruit.

YIELD: 1 cup

Orange Sabayon Sauce

1 egg
3 egg yolks
¾ cup sugar
½ cup dry white wine
¼ cup orange liqueur
½ cup heavy cream,
  optional

In top of double boiler, beat together whole egg, egg yolks, sugar, wine, and liqueur.

Cook over hot water, stirring constantly, until mixture is thick and fluffy. Place top of double boiler in a bowl of ice water. Beat mixture constantly until cold. Refrigerate until ready to serve.

For a creamy sauce, whip ½ cup heavy cream; fold into cooled sauce. Delicious with fruits, crepes, or waffles.

NOTE: Can be refrigerated 2–3 days.

YIELD: 1½ cups

Photo Credits

All photographs used with permission.

Photograph, Page 1:
Hessler Studio of Washington, D.C.

Photograph, Page 10:
U.S. Navy.

Photograph, Page 14, bottom:
Bradley Smith.

Photograph, Page 270, top:
The Kansas City Star.

Photograph, Page 270, bottom:
U.S. Navy.

Photograph, Page 312:
Abbie Rowe, National Park Service.

Photograph, Page 314, top:
Abbie Rowe, National Park Service.

Photograph, Page 314, bottom:
U.S. Army.

All photographs and Mrs. Truman's recipes courtesy of the Harry S. Truman Library.

Special Thanks

Junior Service League of Independence, Missouri would like to acknowledge the following:

Margaret Truman Daniel, for her continuing support of the Junior Service League of Independence.

The Harry S. Truman Library and Museum and staff, for their assistance in compiling the historical information included in this book.

Reathel Odum, personal secretary to Mrs. Truman, for her personal insights and gracious lending of material to further our research.

Audrey Stubbart, for her assistance in completing the historical essay.

A special note of thanks to the many Junior Service League members who contributed their time to make this project successful. It is our hope that the benefits of this labor of love extend to the community we so proudly serve.

Index

Order Blank

The Bess Collection
P.O. Box 1571
Independence, MO 64055

Please send me _____ copies of *The Bess Collection* @ $21.95 per copy ($18.95 plus $3.00 shipping and handling).

Enclosed is my check for $ _____ payable to The Independence Junior Service League or

Charge to Visa( ) or MasterCard ( ) Exp. Date _____

Card # _____

Signature_____

Name _____

Address _____

City _____ State _____ Zip _____

- -

Order Blank

The Bess Collection
P.O. Box 1571
Independence, MO 64055

Please send me _____ copies of *The Bess Collection* @ $21.95 per copy ($18.95 plus $3.00 shipping and handling).

Enclosed is my check for $ _____ payable to The Independence Junior Service League or

Charge to Visa( ) or MasterCard ( ) Exp. Date _____

Card # _____

Signature_____

Name _____

Address _____

City _____ State _____ Zip _____